Old Testament History

Zondervan Quick-Reference Library

ZONDERVAN
QUICK
REFERENCE
LIBRARY

Old Testament History

John H. Sailhamer

ZondervanPublishingHouse
Grand Rapids, Michigan

A Division of HarperCollinsPublishers

Old Testament History
Copyright © 1998 by John H. Sailhamer

Requests for information should be addressed to:

📖 ZondervanPublishingHouse
Grand Rapids, Michigan 49530

Library of Congress Cataloging-in-Publication Data

Sailhamer, John.
   Old Testament history / John H. Sailhamer.
      p. cm. — (Zondervan quick-reference library)
   ISBN: 0-310-20394-5 (softcover)
      1. Bible O.T.—History of Biblical events. 2. Jews—History—To 70 A.D. I. Title.
II. Series.
BS1197.S29 1998
221.9'5-dc 21   97-45989
                                                                              CIP

Interior design by Sue Vandenberg Koppenol

Printed in the United States of America

98 99 00 01 02 03 04 /❖ DC/ 10 9 8 7 6 5 4 3 2 1

Contents

Abbreviations
of the Books of the Bible

Genesis	Gen.	Nahum	Nah.
Exodus	Ex.	Habakkuk	Hab.
Leviticus	Lev.	Zephaniah	Zeph.
Numbers	Num.	Haggai	Hag.
Deuteronomy	Deut.	Zechariah	Zech.
Joshua	Josh.	Malachi	Mal.
Judges	Judg.	Matthew	Matt.
Ruth	Ruth	Mark	Mark
1 Samuel	1 Sam.	Luke	Luke
2 Samuel	2 Sam.	John	John
1 Kings	1 Kings	Acts	Acts
2 Kings	2 Kings	Romans	Rom.
1 Chronicles	1 Chron.	1 Corinthians	1 Cor.
2 Chronicles	2 Chron.	2 Corinthians	2 Cor.
Ezra	Ezra	Galatians	Gal.
Nehemiah	Neh.	Ephesians	Eph.
Esther	Est.	Philippians	Phil.
Job	Job	Colossians	Col.
Psalms	Ps(s).	1 Thessalonians	1 Thess.
Proverbs	Prov.	2 Thessalonians	2 Thess.
Ecclesiastes	Eccl.	1 Timothy	1 Tim.
Song of Songs	Song	2 Timothy	2 Tim.
Isaiah	Isa.	Titus	Titus
Jeremiah	Jer.	Philemon	Philem.
Lamentations	Lam.	Hebrews	Heb.
Ezekiel	Ezek.	James	James
Daniel	Dan.	1 Peter	1 Peter
Hosea	Hos.	2 Peter	2 Peter
Joel	Joel	1 John	1 John
Amos	Amos	2 John	2 John
Obadiah	Obad.	3 John	3 John
Jonah	Jonah	Jude	Jude
Micah	Mic.	Revelation	Rev.

Introduction

What Is the Bible?

One can give different kinds of answers to this question. Our answer here is a simple one: The Bible is a book, or series of books, that boldly tells the story of God's actions in the world. We say "boldly" because what else can we think of someone purporting to tell about God and his ways? Were the Bible not divinely inspired, as it is, its authors would appear presumptuous. Who, for example, would presume to say what God was thinking as he watched Abraham bid farewell to his visitors in Genesis 18:17? Yet the biblical author recounts God's thoughts in as natural a way as telling us that Abraham's visitors "turned away and went toward Sodom" (Gen. 18:22). Both events, the one mundane, the other surely hidden in the deep recesses of the mind of God, make up two simple facts of history. Thus, at its core, the Bible tells a single story about God and humanity and their interaction in history.

As history, the books of the Bible were written over many centuries by authors with vastly different backgrounds and cultures. Many are well known: Moses, David, Solomon, Ezra, Paul. But a surprisingly large number of the biblical authors are nameless. Who wrote the book of Kings, for example, or Chronicles? Who wrote Hebrews? Fortunately, the answer to such questions is not of major consequence in understanding the Bible. While some kinds of books, such as a diary, requires information about its author before it can be properly understood, others are written so that the identity of the author is not needed to understand and appreciate the work.

The fact that the Bible is true and gets its history straight does raise the question, however, of how and where the biblical authors got their information. Though that question has been carefully pursued for centuries, we are in no better position to answer it today than in centuries past. As historians, the biblical writers were hardly interested in telling us how they learned about the past. A few authors tell us of earlier sources they may have used (Num. 21:14), but for the most part, they leave such technical matters behind. Why? The biblical authors are like storytellers of every age—interested primarily in letting the events themselves tell their story. They were writing to common people, not scholars. They took pains to get their facts right, and we are able today to check their accuracy against independent historical sources. But they did not let their desire for accuracy overshadow their task of telling the story.

What Is History?

History is a meaningful account of a series of connected events. An event is something that has happened in time and space. The term *history*, however, is ambiguous. It can be used not only to denote a *flow of events* in time and space, but also *the written record* of that flow.

The study of historical events is as old as the earliest human civilizations. In most early attempts to uncover the past, historians relied heavily on tradition, that is, stories handed down from earlier ages. Modern historiography not only relies on tradition but has also developed more sophisticated tools for reconstructing "the way things were." Its primary procedure to reconstruct past events uses three basic principles: causality, correlation, and analogy.

The principles of *causality* and *correlation* start with the assumption that every historical event is best understood as the result (causality) of a series (correlation) of earlier events. The historian attempts to describe the causes. All historians agree that human events are interrelated and can be understood best by describing the nature of their causal interdependence. Various factors have been suggested for the general flow of historical events. Some suggest, for example, that human events are determined by invariable laws—a view of history called "determinism." The Christian view of historical events is that they are ultimately caused by God's providence. The principle of *analogy* is the code by which the historian draws up a description of a past event. According to this principle, the set of causes used to describe past events must be similar to or analogous to causes of events in the present. We should not expect human affairs to have been any different in the past than they are in the present.

These principles are indispensable for the historian as a tool for reconstructing the past. If we are to understand the events in the Bible as history, we must necessarily employ the tools of causality and analogy. An evangelical approach to the events recorded in the Bible will also employ both the notion of God's providence in explaining the causes of the biblical events and the increasing knowledge of the biblical events gained from ancient records and archaeology. In doing so we are simply following the lead of the biblical writers, whose purpose was to show the hand of God in all the affairs of humanity. An evangelical approach also does not hesitate to use the principle of analogy. To be sure, we do not rule out the possibility of miracles, either for the past or for the present; nevertheless, there is no reason why we cannot seek an explanation for biblical events in the reconstructions of modern archaeologists and historians who used analogy in their reconstructions.

The Bible and History

Few today doubt that the biblical writers set out to record a long, continuous series of historical events. They saw themselves as writing history—recounting the works of God from the earliest days of creation to the last days of the nation of Israel and the founding of the Christian church. The Bible tells a single, if involved, story. Even today, its view of the events it records influences the way secular historians think about the past and the broad scope of world history.

Certainly, it is recognized today that the biblical authors omitted from their accounts most of the history of those peoples and nations who did not come into contact with Israel in the Middle East. There is little in the Bible about China, Japan, and Africa, for example, even though vast civilizations arose in those regions during the period covered by the Bible. The Bible even omits much of the history of those nations who did come into contact with Israel and who played an important role in their national life. What we know in the Bible about Egypt, for example, is only those times and situations when their history intersected with Israel's past. In other words, the aim of the biblical writers was not to give an exhaustive history of the world or of humanity. They wanted to give an account of God's acts with Israel and the early church.

To the extent that past events fell into the service of that goal, be they events in the lives of private individuals or events of global proportions, the biblical writers spared no effort to include them in their works. In the Bible one finds many kinds of historical accounts. There is even an account of the creation of the universe. Few world histories written today venture to begin with creation. But biblical history is all-encompassing. In a real sense, it begins with God alone, recording his first historical act. Nothing is left to one's imagination.

Alongside such epic subjects as Creation, one also finds in the Bible intimate accounts of the lives of private individuals. In the Genesis account of the Flood, for example, we find not only a description of events that could have been known only to an omniscient observer, that is, God, but we also read of the intimate thoughts and feelings of the sole survivor and his family. The Bible is thus "history," but it is a unique kind of history, for its concerns go far beyond the everyday events of human history to include the plans and purposes of God. Because of its wider scope, some have classified Bible history as "holy history," or "salvation history." Others have called it "meta-history" (history that goes far beyond the horizons of ordinary accounts of the past). But for most of the Bible, the simple term "history" fits very well.

History Is Not the Bible

So much attention has been given to the fact that the Bible is history that we often make false assumptions. For example, we may assume that everything that happened to ancient Israel found its way into the Bible and that nothing has been left out. Nothing could be further from the truth. Take the life of the patriarch Abraham as an example: When we meet him, he is already seventy-five years old; we know virtually nothing of his life before that time. Or think of the four hundred years when Israel was in Egypt. What we know about that period has been written on a single page of the Bible. The same can be said of the forty years of Israel's wandering in the desert, or the over four hundred years of the times of the judges. In fact, what we do *not* know about the history of Israel or the early church far exceeds what we do know.

Fortunately, what we do know is given to us in the form of a meaningful story. Thus, we are able to understand what the biblical authors want us to know about the history they record. But we must be careful, as we learn more about Israel's past through archaeology and history, not to allow what we know clearly in the Bible to be overshadowed by what we may learn about Israel's past apart from the Bible. That can lead us to a second false assumption—that whatever we might learn about Israel's past from history or archaeology is automatically a part of the message of the Bible itself.

God has revealed himself in the histories we have in Scripture. Those histories give accurate accounts of what actually happened to Israel and the early church. Yet that does not mean that the more we learn about what actually happened in the past, the more God reveals his truth to us. God's truth for us lies *in the biblical texts* that recount Israel's past. Those texts are inspired and hence are God's means for making known his will to us today. If we could turn the calendar back and set up a video camera at the Red Sea when Israel crossed over it on dry land, we would see the work of God. We would not see, however, the biblical revelation of God's truth for us today, which is found in the Bible, not in the events themselves.

Certainly, most everything the Bible records would be picked up by the video camera. But if we watched only the events and did not read the Bible, we would not see the most appropriate context for understanding those events. We read about the crossing of the Red Sea, for example, within the larger context of the Pentateuch. We can see the thematic links between the biblical account of Creation, the Flood, and the crossing of the Red Sea. In each case God dries up the great sea and allows his people to pass through on dry ground.

Why Study Bible History?

If all we need to know about Israel's past is given us in the Bible, why should we study anything more than what we have in the Bible itself? The most important answer to that question, of course, is that if we want to understand what God teaches us today in the Bible, then reading and studying the Bible make sense as it is. We do not need to learn more about Israel's past or the history of the early church to understand it more deeply or more correctly. Having said that, however, it is also important to say that the study of biblical history is essential in its own right. There are at least two reasons that make it so.

(1) A knowledge of the history of Israel both in and apart from the Bible is essential for demonstrating the truthfulness of the biblical message. The Bible claims to be true. It does so by claiming to be historically accurate. But how can we know it is historically accurate without knowing a great deal about the history it professes to recount? Before the rise of historical research and our modern ability to reconstruct a great deal of historical information about the distant past, readers of the Bible were more or less constrained to take the Bible at its own word. It was reasoned that the Bible must be true because it was God's Word, and if it was God's Word, it must be true. One can easily see the circularity of reasoning involved. But there was little opportunity to do more in defense of the truthfulness of the Bible. Today the situation is much different, for we now have independent historical means to test the accuracy of the Bible. What is more, we have historical tools to test it in some amazingly intricate details. In Genesis 37:28, for example, we are told that Joseph was sold into service in Egypt for "twenty shekels of silver." Is that a historically accurate statement? Absolutely! We know from contemporary records that servants in that region of the world were sold for twenty shekels of silver. We also know that the price fluctuated and that only in Joseph's day was the price twenty shekels. Such knowledge can thus confirm the historical accuracy of the biblical stories.

(2) A knowledge of biblical history can also help fill in the details of many stories in the Bible. Before the rise of historical science, Bible readers assumed that biblical characters looked and lived much like people in their own day. In medieval paintings, for example, David is often pictured living in a medieval, European castle and wearing medieval armor. Through archaeology, paintings, and language studies, however, we get a much better picture of how Bible people lived in their everyday lives and how they interacted with other people.

Primeval History

The Bible and Prehistory

The events described in the first few chapters of the Bible pose particular questions about the exact nature of biblical history. What, in fact, can we call the type of narrative in Genesis 1 and 2? An increasing number of biblical scholars find themselves today looking for a more adequate way to describe the literary and historical intent of the creation account. They are reluctant to read those narratives as historical accounts. If read as a literal history, they believe, the creation narrative radically conflicts with our modern scientific view of the origin of the world. They are, rightly or wrongly, convinced that a historical reading teaches that the earth and the universe are only a few thousand years old, that the whole of the universe was created in six days, and that the sun, moon, and stars were not formed until the fourth day—two days before human beings were created. One has to admit that if such were the case, it would fundamentally conflict with our modern understanding of the world.

It is thus not surprising that one often hears expressions such as "poetry-like" and "meta-history" to describe the nature of these early Genesis narratives. If these narratives were, in fact, "poetry-like," we might be able to read them less literally. We might be able to look for truth in them apart from what they appear to be saying about the days of creation and the age of the universe. But there are serious problems with the notion that Genesis 1 is "poetry-like." There is, in fact, little in the text that supports reading it even "like" poetry. We know from clear examples in the Bible what biblical poetry looks like—and Genesis 1 does not follow that pattern. One only has to look at a biblical poetic description of creation, such as Job 38, where God is pictured as a carpenter making a house and then as a parent caring for a child, to see that Genesis 1 is not poetic. It presents no such images of God. It reads as narrative, and when we read these verses, we are led to believe that they depict reality for us in literal and realistic terms.

Surely the narratives of Genesis 1 and 2 are highly stylized and show many signs of being shaped and artfully composed. That, however, does not make them poetry, nor does it make them "poetry-like." Virtually all biblical narratives are shaped and artfully composed. It may be convenient to dismiss the historical intent of the author of Genesis 1 and 2 as less than literal or figurative, but it is all but impossible to do so on the basis of what we find in the texts themselves. We may safely assume, then, that the author of Genesis 1 and 2 saw himself as writing real history. Certainly his subject matter was unique; nevertheless, he intended it to be taken as fact, not fiction.

Is Genesis 1 and 2 History?

We believe that a straightforward reading of Genesis 1 and 2 gives every impression that the events happened precisely as they are described. The author has intended them to be read both realistically and literally. Moreover, Genesis 1 has been taken at face value as describing historical events by virtually all its readers for most of its history. Even those who in the past rejected the plain meaning of the text in favor of finding a "spiritual truth" hidden in its words admitted that its "plain meaning" was literal and historical. Genesis 1 is presented as a story—a story that gives no hint that it is not also a true story, in the sense of being a literal depiction of what actually happened.

Further support for our understanding of Genesis 1 and 2 as actual history is the fact that the narrative form of these chatpers does not differ from the rest of biblical narrative texts. Its patterns and narrative structures occur with equal frequency in the narratives of Israel's stay in Egypt and their wandering in the desert. They are likewise the same as those in the later biblical narratives of David, Solomon, and the kings of Israel and Judah. If we take those narratives as realistic and literal, as most biblical historians do, then there is little basis for not doing so in Genesis 1 and 2. Both texts have an equal share of miraculous events, so that both are not easily susceptible to the usual forms of historical investigation. But that fact should not be taken as indicating that they are not intended to record realistic and literal historical accounts. The historical problem lies in what they are attempting to describe, namely, miraculous events.

Having said that, we can readily acknowledge that Genesis 1 is a unique historical narrative. It is unique, however, by virtue of its subject matter, not its form. Genesis 1 is a history about a unique event—creation. Usually when we talk about history and historical events, we have in mind events that correspond to our own experiences of life. For us, the past is linked to the present and therefore shares certain basic features with our present world. There is, in other words, a meaningful analogy between our world and events in the past. But in the historical events recorded in Genesis 1, we are taken into a world that is greater than our own everyday world. Here we read about things that we have no other means of knowing. It takes us beyond the boundaries of our historical and scientific knowledge—and it does so literally and realistically. We are given, clearly and simply, God's perspective on this most important of historical events.

The "Days" of Creation

Are the "days" in Genesis 1 to be taken literally? That question can be answered in several ways. Some maintain that the "days" need not be understood as actual twenty-four-hour days. The sunrise that begins each "day" is merely a symbolic depiction of a real event but not a literal one. Others insist that the creation narrative is to be taken realistically and literally. As such, the narrative is also historical. That means we can understand it by analogies from our own experience. The "days" of Genesis 1 are thus real and literal twenty-four-hour days, but they depict events that lie outside our everyday experience. That first week was a real and literal week, one like we ourselves experience every seven days. At the same time, that first week was not merely like any other week, for God did an extraordinary work in that week. Thus the events of the week far transcend anything that has occurred since.

If the Genesis account was merely historical in the sense that all other humans events are historical, we would have to find analogies of creation in our everyday world. That is, we should be able to find actual instances of creation in our present world. If we could do that, creation would not be a unique event and would, in fact, not be the kind of creation described in Genesis 1, namely, creation out of nothing. By identifying God's act of creation with an element or a feature of our own experience of the world, we lose sight of the actual work of God in creation. The biblical account of creation is specifically designed to take us out of our everyday present world and put us back into the world at the beginning of time. We thereby come to see our world as a product of God's direct action. The world becomes for us a divine artifact. Viewed in that manner, the biblical account of creation leads us to study the universe as God's creation. We see our world as God's world, and we see the handiwork of God in that world.

The Bible, Science, and History

Technically, science has little or nothing to say about the ultimate origin of the universe. Its domain is the everyday affairs of the physical universe. History also is about the everyday affairs of human beings (past and present). Both history and science attempt to explain the world by appealing to basic laws of observation. Both these disciplines are explainable in terms of general laws. Creation, of necessity, lies outside the application of those laws. Who has ever observed a creation? A basic law of science and history is that "something cannot come from nothing." But in creation, that is precisely what must happen: "Something comes from nothing."

Creation is a central concern of the Bible. Its story (history) begins with the divine act of creation. A basic tenet of the Bible, therefore, is that "something has come from nothing," that the universe was created *ex nihilo* (out of nothing). The Bible does not teach that creation happens all the time. To that extent it agrees with science. But the Bible does state that if God wills, he can do so again. It thus makes statements that claim to be true about creation, about history, and about science. In making such statements, however, the Bible lies outside the range of either the natural or the physical world.

Science and history, on the other hand, claim only to make statements about the natural and physical world. As such, both history and science renounce any claims to speak about creation. When they make their observations, scientists and historians are working within their own domains. On this level, there is little room for conflict between history, science, and the Bible; the Bible merely takes a more comprehensive view of the world.

The observations of scientists and historians, however, are often based on assumptions they make about the world—assumptions that are not grounded in observation. For example, many scientists assume that the material world is without a beginning and end (materialism). When scientists or historians make assumptions of that kind, they necessarily cross over outside the domain of science and into the domain of the biblical creation stories, which speaks directly about the reality that existed "before" the past and the present. There is no physical evidence that the universe is eternal. Moreover, when a scientist states that the universe is eternal, he or she does so at the expense of the claims of Scripture. A scientist has every right to make such an assumption and thus contradict Scripture, but it should be acknowledged that it is an assumption.

Biblical Theism, Materialism, and Naturalism

Is it possible to harmonize the views of the Bible with those of science? We believe the resolution of that conflict should not come from showing the Bible to be more scientific than science or more historical than history. Both approaches, incidentally, have been widely used by evangelical biblical scholars and scientists. The resolution should, rather, come from showing that the assumptions being laid down by the Bible are more valid assumptions about the world than those laid down by either modern science or modern historiography. The assumptions about God and the world laid down in the Bible are called *theism*, whereas the assumptions of science are called *materialism*, and those of history, *naturalism*. These are, of course, philosophical questions and should be treated at that level.

Theism is the belief in a creator God, who is transcendent over (not a part of) and governor of the material universe. The fact that God is the creator means that only he is eternal. The material world he created and governs thus had a beginning and, if he so wills, will have an end. In theism, God is active not only in creation but continues to be involved in the world. A theistic view of scientific matters allows for miracles; and a theistic view of history allows for providence, God's active control of the events of history.

Materialism is the belief that all reality exists in the form of matter and energy. The world can and should be explained solely on the basis of the interaction of these two elements.

Naturalism is the belief that the only forces at work in the world are those inherent in the physical world, including the active role of human will. History must be explained solely in those terms. There is no place for the activity of a transcendent God.

Throughout the Bible statements are made that claim to be historically true. For the most part, those claims involve the actions of God in history. The divine act of creation is itself a unique instance of God's activity with respect to the physical world and history. By initiating history, that is, by creating human beings, God became involved in history. There are, however, many other examples of God's acts in history that are recorded in the Bible. God parted the Red Sea (Ex. 14), for example, and God raised Jesus from the dead. There are many areas, then, in which the Bible may find itself in conflict with the naturalism of modern historiography. Furthermore, in the parting of the Red Sea or the turning of the Nile into blood (Ex. 7), the Bible is also in conflict with the materialism of modern science. Our particular interest here is with the relationship between the Bible, science, and history in the early chapters of Genesis.

Creationism and Evolution

Evangelicals have typically taken one of three positions when confronted with the possibility of conflict between the Bible and science in the early chapters of Genesis:

(1) *Creationism.* According to modern creationists, the biblical account of creation in Genesis 1 is to be interpreted literally to mean God created the universe in six days. He created man and woman on the sixth day. The universe is, thus, young—only about ten thousand years old. Modern creationists usually hold that the present condition of the earth, which gives an appearance of being much older, reflects the catastrophic destruction wrought by the Flood. "Flood geology" is the notion that geological formations and fossil deposits are best explained in terms of the effects of the Flood rather than as remnants of the original creation.

(2) *Progressive creationism.* According to progressive creationism, God created the universe in the beginning—some eight to fifteen billion years ago. Moreover, life on earth began nearly three and a half billion years ago. The biblical account of Adam and Eve is historical and can be dated prior to the first traces of human life, about twenty to fifty thousand years ago. God personally created the first man and woman; they did not evolve from primates. The account of creation in Genesis 1 is not taken in a strictly literal fashion. Either the days are to be taken as long ages of time, or the whole of the account is to be understood as a sort of picturesque story that teaches about a real act of God but does not give a literal depiction of those acts.

(3) *Theistic evolution.* According to most versions of theistic evolution, God created the universe and all life, using the process of evolution and natural selection. The biblical account of creation is understood merely as a picturesque way to portray the fact that God was behind the evolutionary process of creation.

Theistic evolutionists, like progressive creationists, do not take a literal view of Genesis 1. They, in fact, often scorn such a view as obscurantism. The narrative of Genesis 1 is meant to be read merely as a story, telling us that God created the world but not how he did it. For the how we must go to science. To this extent, progressive creationists and theistic evolutionists are similar, though they disagree on their assessment of the validity of the theory of evolution. Most progressive creationists retain some degree of literal meaning in Genesis 1.

In another regard, theistic evolutionists are also similar in their approach to creationists. Both view the meaning of the biblical account in terms of their own particular scientific understanding of the world. The theistic evolutionists apply their evolutionary theories to Genesis 1, and the creationists read Genesis 1 in light of their view of the Genesis Flood. In both cases the meaning of the Bible is "explained" and shown to be true by scientific laws and theory.

The Age of the Universe

A key issue in the interpretation of Genesis 1 is the question of what the chapter implies about the age of the universe. Early biblical chronologies uniformly assumed the world was created only a few thousand years ago. According to traditional Judaism, the year 1995 is 5,755 years after the creation. In the seventeenth century, Bishop Usher dated creation at 4004 B.C.

Such attempts at an absolute chronology of the world were not based as much on Genesis 1 as on the genealogies of Genesis 5 and 10. The addition of the respective ages of the men in those genealogies—the number of years between Adam and Noah, and between Noah and Abraham—was taken as the total number of years since the creation. Such an approach to dating the time of creation is based on two faulty assumptions: that the biblical genealogies are to be understood as strict chronologies, and that the "beginning" of creation (Gen. 1:1) occurred on the first day of the week recounted in that chapter (1:2–31). Many English translations, in fact, have rendered the summary in 1:5 as "and there was evening, and there was morning—the first day" (NIV). In the phrase "the first day" is an implicit assumption that there were no other days preceding this one. The Hebrew text of that passage, however, does not have the word "first." It simply reads, "and there was evening, and there was morning—one day." The first day of that week, in other words, was not the first day of creation. It was simply "one day." Such an understanding of the text allows for a considerable amount of time for a chronology of creation.

In the current debate, all sides now generally recognize that the genealogies in Genesis 5 and 10 are not intended as strict chronologies. Creationists, however, are generally not willing to expand the length of time covered by the chronologies indefinitely, as are progressive creationists. Creationists believe in a "young earth," that is, a creation that is only a few thousand years old (see previous section).

As Christians have debated the chronology of creation, the question of the age of the universe has also become the center of a vigorous discussion among scientists, particularly astrophysicists involved with the Hubble space telescope. While not long ago it was generally argued that the age of the universe was about fifteen billion years old, it is now thought to be only half that old, about eight billion years. Using new measurements from the Hubble telescope, scientists have been able to determine that the speed with which the universe is now drifting apart is considerably greater than previously assumed. This higher speed for the expansion of the universe means less time for it to have expanded to its present shape.

The Origin of Life

When did life on this planet begin? Did simple forms of life develop into more complex forms and eventually into human life as we know it today? These are not questions raised only by biblical creationists these days. Though many modern scientists do not accept the creationists' interpretations of Genesis 1, they do agree with them that classical theories of the origin of life, such as Darwinian evolution, are in serious need of reassessment.

In classical evolutionary theory, life began spontaneously on this planet billions of years ago. It began in simple, single-cell forms, and over long periods of time gradually evolved into more complex forms, eventually reaching animal and human life. This theory allows virtually unlimited time for the formation of life on earth. But as new methods of research have clarified some of the basic questions, problems have surfaced for this theory.

To take one example, the amount time for life to develop on earth has now become impossibly small. In its initial stages, the earth was extremely hot and was repeatedly bombarded by asteroids, which tended to maintain that high temperature. These bombardments acted in the same way as keeping the burner on a stove keeps a boiling pot hot. The earth could begin to cool only after the asteroids gradually ceased to rain upon the earth's surface. Scientists now realize that the earth could not have cooled sufficiently for life to exist until about 3.8 billion years ago. It is true, at least theoretically, that the number of years between the cooling of the earth and the present could reasonably accommodate the development of life—though there was not much time to spare. Microscopic examinations of the earliest rock formations, however, have recently revealed fossils of highly complex microorganisms, dated between 3.46 and 3.47 billion years ago—just after the earth had cooled sufficiently to support life. These were, for all intents and purposes, modern forms of life. The few hundred million years between the time when the earth cooled (3.8 billion years ago) and the existence of these complex forms of life (3.5 billion years ago) is too short a time period to support modern scientific theories of the origin of life on earth.

In light of such discoveries, some scientists now suggest that the evolutionary process was perhaps not as slow as was previously supposed. In a friendly environment like earth, they say, early life-forms would have flourished at a more rapid rate. Some scientists have even suggested that life itself could have developed, even into complex forms, literally overnight.

The Origin of Human Life

Both the Bible and modern science place the origin of actual human life (homo sapiens) very late on the geological clock. When reckoned by strict archaeological evidence, human beings begin to show up only about thirty thousand years ago. Compared to the millions of years all other species of life have existed on earth, human beings arrived only yesterday.

When genetic codes of human beings are examined, the time at which they appear to have arrived on the scene is slightly earlier: 200,000–270,000 years ago. Both time periods are remarkably surprising for an evolutionary theory of human origin. The study of the genetic codes of our male and female ancestors also reveals that all human beings alive today can be traced back to a single male and female. Though all forms of life on earth, human and otherwise, have the same basic genetic code, there are vast differences among the higher forms of life, differences that produce the immense varieties of life we see on earth. That is, the difference between an elephant and a gnat lies only in a small percentage of their total genetic makeup.

But in spite of the great similarities in genetic structure between humans and the rest of the animal chain, there appear to be no immediate or distant genetic ancestors to modern humans. The notion that human beings evolved from a specific lower form of "human," or subhuman, life has therefore become a problematic notion. There are, in fact, today no inherently plausible evolutionary explanations for the origin of human beings. They suddenly arrive on the scene, late in the process, fully developed and capable at their earliest stages of producing advanced forms of culture and societies. Earlier ape-like creatures inhabited the earth for hundreds of thousands of years, and, indeed, many of them still exist today as chimpanzees and gorillas. Genetically, however, none of those creatures bears any close or inherent relationship to human beings today. As the cave paintings in Western Europe demonstrate, already thirty thousand years ago human beings were as culturally and spiritually advanced as they are today.

To say that science does not have a plausible explanation for the origin of human beings is not to say that the biblical explanation is therefore true. It does, however, cast a considerably different sort of light on the biblical account, in which God fashioned the first man from the soil of the ground (Gen. 2:7) and the first woman from his side (2:22). One can only conclude that those accounts are intended to be taken as an actual record of how God created the man and woman. As far as the biblical historians are concerned, the fashioning of man from the ground (Gen. 2:7) is no more or less miraculous than the parting of the Red Sea (Ex. 14) or the resurrection of Christ.

The Genesis Account of Creation

Genesis 1 and 2, the account of creation, records two primary works of God. Genesis 1:1 recounts his creation of the universe. The expression "heavens and earth," or more properly, "sky and land," is a figure of speech that refers to all that exists—the universe as we know it, including the sun, moon, and stars. According to this verse, all these things were created "in the beginning." The Hebrew term "beginning" refers to an indefinite period of time. The text, thus, does not say God created the universe in a single instance, but over a long period of time.

In Genesis 1:2 the creation narrative makes a major shift in focus, turning the reader's attention to the condition of "the land" as God begins to prepare it for the man and woman. What does "land" mean in this narrative? Most English translations see this as the whole "earth," but the Hebrew expression more likely refers only to the Promised Land. Throughout the Pentateuch, the biblical writer's primary focus is on the land promised to Abraham (15:18), the land God was to give to his descendants, the nation of Israel. Already here the writer wants us to see that God specifically prepared the Promised Land as the place of his blessing (1:28).

In the week recorded in Genesis 1:2–2:4, God carefully prepares the land. He separates the waters that cover it and makes the dry land appear. He plants fruit trees, which are to be for humankind's nourishment. He populates the land with all kinds of animals.

What does God do on the fourth day? Seeing that those heavenly bodies have already been created in Genesis 1:1, God's work on the fourth day most likely consists of his making a formal declaration of purpose for having created these heavenly bodies "in the beginning." God announces that the heavenly luminaries are to be for signs and seasons—reminders of God's power and glory and calendars to mark the periods of the year. Technically, the word "seasons" refers to those times of the year when Israel was to come together at the temple to worship God.

The story of Israel's history in the Bible thus begins with God's preparation of the "good land" for his chosen people. When God later commanded them to go into the land and possess it, he cast out those who were then living there and gave it to his people. But when Israel disobeyed God and followed after the gods of the other peoples, God also cast them out of the land. According to Genesis 1 and 2, it was God's land, and he could give it to whom he pleased. We also see that biblical history is moving toward a goal, one that will be realized in Revelation 20–22, where God's people once again live in the Promised Land and enjoy God's blessings.

Early Human Society

In its account of early human society, the Bible covers a vast amount of history in a relatively brief number of pages. That history is a selective one. For the most part, it covers only that line of Adam's descendants that culminates in the family of Noah.

Genesis 4 contains a brief account of the civilization founded by Cain in the land of Nod, a land east of the Promised Land and in the same general location as the city of Babylon in Genesis 11. There Cain and his descendants built the first recorded city and invented the primary features of human civilization: raising livestock, dwelling in tents, making musical instruments, and working with metal. Since that civilization was wiped out by the Flood in Noah's day, the writer spares little time on it. His purpose in pointing to the achievements of that lost civilization was, apparently, to highlight the magnitude of the destruction of the Flood.

Needless to say, the Flood recounted in Genesis 6–9 represents the most crucial event within the early history of humanity. The Bible presents it as a global flood, whose magnitude staggers the imagination. If we take the Bible seriously on this issue, we cannot hope to learn much about human history before that Flood. Many "flood geologists" attribute the present geological conditions on earth to the catastrophic effects of that Flood.

What concerns us most here is the extent to which effects of the Flood may influence our understanding of early human remains. It is well known, for example, that traces of early human remains scattered throughout the world appear quite suddenly about thirty thousand years ago. Though we are accustomed to thinking of those remains in light of the early, preflood civilizations, it may be more accurate to relate them to the time after the Flood. As suggested above, unless the Flood was only a local phenomenon, its effect would have largely removed any evidence of earlier cultures, so that most of human remains throughout the world should be related to the families that followed the Flood—the descendents of Shem, Ham, and Japheth. According to the biblical account, all known peoples on earth have descended from Noah and his three sons. Those sons and their descendants fanned out from the resting place of the ark in three directions: The sons of Shem went east, the sons of Ham went south, and the sons of Japheth spread west. The Bible does not intend to say that these were the only directions and locations populated by Noah's sons. The biblical account is a highly selected version of the actual process of the repopulation of the earth after the Flood.

Patriarchal History

Abraham

Beginning in Genesis 12, the Bible takes a decided turn in its focus on historical events. World history fades into the background of the biblical narratives, and only occasionally are events of global importance recorded (cf. Gen. 14). For the most part, the focus centers on the lives of certain key individuals and their families—the first of whom was Abraham.

Abraham was born in the twenty-second century B.C. During that time, the great Akkad empire in Mesopotamia was coming to an end. Political power in both Canaan and Egypt were fragmenting. We first meet Abraham in the city of "Ur of the Chaldeans"—a major city occupied by the Babylonians, that is, the Chaldeans. Perhaps the biblical author wants us to identify the city of Ur with the city of Babylon, mentioned in Genesis 10:10; 11:1–9. If so, then Abraham's leaving Ur of the Chaldeans and traveling westward to the Promised Land is linked to God's forced return of the people of that city back into the land, as 11:8 suggests: "The LORD scattered them from there over all the face of all the land" (NIV, earth). On his way to the Promised Land, Abraham first settled in a region in northern Mesopotamia called Haran, where he remained until the death of his father. The Lord then called on him to leave his family and continue his journey to the Promised Land (cf. Acts 7:2).

Abraham was seventy-five years old when he entered the land. Recent studies of seasonal agricultural changes suggests that the migration of Abraham may have been associated with a more general migration of peoples throughout the Near East as a result of widespread famine. In fact, Abraham himself felt forced to travel beyond Canaan into Egypt because of famine (Gen. 12:10). He entered Egypt during its First Intermediate Period, a time of great social unrest. After a brief sojourn there, he settled in the land of Canaan as a farmer and shepherd. While there, he was called on to defend its inhabitants against a cruel attack by four kings from the east, who had formed a coalition to launch a military raid against the cities of Canaan. The purpose of the raid was to loot and pillage the region. Abraham, more or less a cultural outcast at the time and hence called a "Hebrew" (most likely meaning "outcast"), rallied his own household of 318 men and defeated the eastern kings as they fled. Such international conflicts and raiding parties were a common fact of life throughout the Near East in Abraham's day.

The biblical writer uses the account of Abraham's victory as a picture of the Lord's blessing of Abraham. Just as God delivered Canaan through the house of Abraham, God would also, in the future, deliver all the nations from the curse of the Fall. God sealed his promise to bless the nations in Abraham by entering a solemn oath with him.

Isaac

The Bible devotes little attention to the events in the life of Isaac. And in the events that are recorded, only a few details are given. But these details are essential to the development of the basic themes of the book. Since a central theme of the Bible is the promise to Abraham that his descendants would become a great nation, much attention is given to the birth of Isaac and to the search for his wife, Rebecca.

Isaac was born after Abraham had lived in Canaan for over two decades. Isaac's wife, however, came from Abraham's relatives in Haran. In typical Near Eastern fashion, Abraham sent out his trusted servant to search for a bride for his son. When he found her, he brought her back to Isaac in Canaan. Thus the people of God, as the Bible sees it, did not come from the inhabitants of Canaan, nor did they gain possession of the land through family ties. They had no natural rights to it. Their dwelling in the land of Canaan was based solely on God's promise to Abraham.

Jacob

With the birth of the third generation of Abraham, Jacob and Esau, a new element is introduced into the biblical story—conflict within the family of Abraham. Jacob struggled with his brother Esau in the same way that their descendants, Israel and Edom, later struggled in the land. It was, in fact, the result of the struggle between Jacob and Esau that forced Jacob to leave the land of Canaan and seek a home with his mother's family in Haran. While living there, Jacob met and married two sisters—Leah, the older one, whom he was tricked by his father-in-law into marrying, and Rachel, her younger and more beautiful sister.

The struggle that characterized Jacob's relationships within his family were mirrored in the political events of his day. In Mesopotamia, the kingdom of Mari in the northwest and Babylon in the south were beginning to defend themselves through alliances with the many city-states throughout the Near East. Political power was beginning to assert itself in Canaan too in a close-knit alliance of city-states. Egypt had also been reunited under the rule of a series of powerful dynasties. The struggles that ultimately marred the relations between the sons of Jacob can thus be seen within the context of a growing assertion of power throughout the entire region.

What is remarkable about the biblical accounts of those struggles is the way in which God used them to further his own covenant promises. Conflict sent Jacob into Mesopotamia to seek a wife. Conflict sent Joseph into Egypt where, years later, the entire promised seed of Abraham was saved from famine. The biblical writer wants to show that God's promises are not limited or thwarted by human conflict, be it within God's own people or on a global scale. Joseph's final words to this brothers at the conclusion of the book of Genesis serve as a fitting conclusion to the events and struggles of the lives of the patriarchs: "You intended to harm me, but God intended it for good to accomplish what is now being done, the saving of many lives" (Gen. 50:20).

Israel in Egypt and the Exodus

Israel in Egypt

The story of Joseph (Gen. 37–50) records how the family of Israel came into a permanent sojourn in Egypt. As in the account of the life of Jacob, the Joseph story depicts a sovereign, faithful God working out his plan among his chosen people and among the nations of the world. God used the nations both to preserve and to punish his people.

Though the details of the account are clear, we have only the biblical chronology to place these events within the larger framework of world history. Apart from the Bible, there is no mention of Joseph or his ascendancy to power in Egypt. Like most ancient peoples, however, Egyptian records were highly selective and incomplete. According to the chronology maintained throughout Genesis, Joseph entered Egypt in 1876 B.C.—that is, during the last years of its Middle Kingdom period. The pharaoh at that time was Sesostris III, the greatest king of this period. One of his most notable achievements, according to Egyptian records, was a nationwide administrative reform that took the power away from local feudal lords by establishing a centralized administrative head, second only to the pharaoh himself.

Such events fit the biblical stories remarkably well (cf. Gen. 47:13–26). Order was restored throughout Egypt, and there was great need for centralizing food supplies during years of high productivity. At the time the early Babylonian empire flourished in Mesopotamia under the reign of King Hammurapi, and Egyptian records mention foreign rulers. Those rulers, called the Hyksos, were apparently from the same groups of people from which the patriarchs ultimately derived. Many of them had names that resemble those of the patriarchs.

Some early biblical scholars hypothesized that the Hyksos kings in Egypt were the descendants of Joseph, who ruled Egypt after him. What makes that an unlikely hypothesis, however, is the fact that the Hyksos were driven out of Egypt long before the time of the Exodus. But the fact that non-Egyptians ruled in Egypt during the time of Joseph shows that the story of Joseph is not only inherently plausible but, on the face of it, likely.

Exodus 1 gives a list of seventy names of those who accompanied Joseph into Egypt. That number increased greatly during the four hundred years that Israel lived there. According to 1:8, a "new king" arose in Egypt, who did not acknowledge the special status awarded to Israel in Joseph's day. This new king perhaps represents a change in dynastic rule. If so, it was most likely the first king of the eighteenth dynasty, Ahmose (ca. 1567 B.C.). Note the last element in his name, *mose*. Many Egyptian pharaohs during this period had that element in their names— the same element as the name "Moses."

Life and Oppression in Egypt

The statement that the new king "did not know about Joseph" (Ex. 1:8) suggests that Israel was no longer awarded special status in Egypt (cf. Gen. 46:31–34). From then on, the Israelites were as suspect as any other group of foreign people living there. Thus, the Egyptian king decided to prevent the Israelites from using their bulging population to gain independence. That this king was concerned about the Israelites' possibly leaving the land suggests that they were already in service to the Egyptians before the severe oppression began. This is consistent with what we know about ancient Egypt, for all Egypt was, in effect, in service to the king. Any foreigners who entered the land of Egypt as a matter of course were incorporated into some sort of service. Thus, the new pharaoh did not so much initiate Israel's bondage as made their bondage oppressive and attempted to weaken their will to resist.

The first measure the king took proved unsuccessful, for the Israelites increased in strength and number rather than decreased (Ex. 1:12). His next measure attempted to halt the births of all male Israelite children: The Hebrew midwives were instructed to kill every male child but let the female children live (1:16). That plan also backfired because the Hebrew midwives feared God and refused to obey the king. The final, most desperate, measure was the king's order to kill every Israelite boy by casting him into the Nile River (1:22).

That measure too, in the long run, failed. Exodus 2 records what Moses' parents did to protect their newborn son from the decree of the pharaoh, hiding him for three months. When he could no longer be hidden, Moses' mother constructed a small reed basket and placed him in the basket and in the Nile River. There is a clear irony in the account of Moses' rescue. Though his parents did not fulfill the full intent of the pharaoh by casting him into the Nile, they did put him into the Nile in a basket and, by that means, saved his life. Moreover, because they put him into the Nile, he was later found by the pharaoh's own daughter and brought up in Pharaoh's house. God was providentially watching over his people. Historical events reveal his plan and purpose.

When Moses came of age, he became aware of his true identity and felt compassion on his Israelite brothers because of the hard labor they were forced to perform. Coming to the aid of another Israelite being beaten by an Egyptian, Moses fatally struck the Egyptian, killed him, and then fled into the desert. It was there that God called Moses to deliver Israel from Egypt.

The Call of Moses

The event recorded in Exodus 2:23 marks a crucial transition in biblical history. A new king had arisen in Egypt, and it was thus possible for Moses to return to his people. It was, in fact, customary for new kings to pardon those who had fled the country during the oppressive reigns of their predecessors. The reign of a new king was often marked by a great homecoming. But there was more to these events than ancient custom. The biblical writer reminds us that God was also at work here. The Israelites were still suffering from their oppression and had cried out to him for help (2:24). God heard their cry and set out to call Moses into his service to deliver his people from the hand of the Egyptians. God's actions in intervening on Israel's behalf were motivated by his faithfulness to his covenant with Abraham (2:24).

For some time already, God had set Moses apart and prepared him for the task of deliverer. As God's plan now rolled into action, Moses was brought into the picture. From a burning bush God called him and told him precisely what he was to do: to go before the Egyptian king, demand the release of the Israelite slaves, and from those released captives form a nation (3:7–8). Moses immediately grasped the magnitude of God's commission and asked, in apparent unbelief, "Who am I to do such a thing?" This was not an expression of fear so much as it was a recognition that he, a mere commoner, and a shepherd at that, had no right or opportunity to appear before Pharaoh and make such demands. Moses knew that he could expect no official recognition among the Egyptians, much less the pharaoh himself.

But God responded to Moses with the assurance that he would be with Moses and would provide that recognition by signs and wonders he would perform through Moses. Moses realized that God's task would meet stiff opposition in Egypt, the nature of which was to be theological. By what grounds could he make demands of the pharaoh and expect even his own people to accept his leadership? Only by clearly explaining to the people something of the nature and purpose of the God who was calling him. When Moses asked the name of God (Ex. 3:13), therefore, he was asking more than merely God's identity. He was asking a question about the very nature of God himself. In the ancient world, a name expressed the very nature of its bearer. In addition to the promise of his presence and help signified in his name, God also gave to Moses three physical signs to perform for the people to show that God had sent him. Moses' staff became a snake (4:2–5); his hand became white with leprosy and then well again (4:6–7); and water from the Nile River became red with blood (4:9). When the people saw these signs, they believed God had sent Moses (4:31).

The Exodus From Egypt

In Exodus 7:3–5 God told Moses that he would harden Pharaoh's heart in order that he might send signs and wonders upon Egypt. These signs (the ten plagues) were to demonstrate God's power to the Egyptians and to the Israelites. In many respects, the plagues were directed against specific features of the Egyptians' conception of the world. For them, the entire universe was to exist as a harmonious whole, with each part well balanced within that whole. Such a well-balanced universe they called *ma'at*. It was the chief responsibility of the king, as the incarnate god on earth, to maintain and preserve that balance. In the plagues, this balanced world became systematically and deliberately disrupted, and the pharaoh was powerless to protect it.

Thus, the plagues unmasked the Egyptian king's claims to deity and to maintain the order of the world. The king had, in effect, taken credit for something that he had no part in. The plagues demonstrated publicly how false his claims were. God alone has power over the universe. Not only does he maintain its order and balance, but if he chooses, he may also throw it completely back into a state of chaos. Ultimately, the plagues led up to the final plague, the death of the firstborn, especially the firstborn of Pharaoh. Pharaoh's firstborn son was, in fact, thought to be the next incarnate god. But that son, along with all the other firstborn, was taken by the death angel sent from God.

Biblical chronology suggests that the pharaoh of the Exodus (1440 B.C.) was Amenhotep II (1450–1425 B.C.). The king who followed him was his son Thutmosis IV. According to the biblical account, Thutmosis IV would not have been the firstborn of Pharaoh. It is interesting to note that ancient Egyptian records also suggest that Thutmosis IV was not the firstborn son of Amenhotep II. Historians, in fact, believe Thutmosis IV rose to the throne through "an unforeseen turn of fate, such as the premature death of an elder brother" (*Cambridge Ancient History*, 2:321).

The last plague has been memorialized in the Bible by the celebration of the Passover. On the night of the Exodus, the Israelites were required by God to slaughter an unblemished lamb and spread its blood over the doorposts of their houses. In those houses so marked by the blood, the life of the firstborn was spared. Henceforth in Israel, the celebration of the Passover meal reminded the people of God's gracious salvation and deliverance of Israel.

The Crossing of the Red Sea

The exact location of the Red Sea at the time of the Exodus is uncertain. Attempts have been made to identify the various locations mentioned in Exodus 13 and 14 (Ethan, Succoth, Pi Hahiroth, Migdol, and Baal Zephon), but these still remain provisional.

The most important location, of course, is that of the "Red Sea" itself. The Hebrew name of this body of water is, in fact, not the "Red Sea," but the "Sea of Reeds." The Hebrew term translated "reeds" or "rushes" is, apparently, a loanword borrowed from Egyptian. Unfortunately, the name "Sea of Reeds" for the body of water that Israel crossed often leads to the erroneous conclusion that the Israelites crossed only a low marshland partially dried up by a strong wind. The problem with that interpretation is that the term "Sea of Reeds" is used in a much broader sense throughout the biblical text. The term is, in fact, used for the whole area of water included in the modern "Red Sea." That is why early versions of the Bible called the "Sea of Reeds" by the modern name, "Red Sea." If we then take the modern location of the Red Sea as our starting point, the other locations visited by the Israelites on their Exodus journey are not difficult to identify. Those sites are, for the most part, located around the northern tip of the present day Red Sea, east of the delta region of the Nile and along what is today the Suez Canal.

The biblical historian is clear that it was unnecessary for the Israelites to cross the Red Sea in order to flee Egypt. Other routes were available. But God led them to the Red Sea as another occasion for him to reveal his sovereign power over Egypt and the nations (Ex. 14:2–4).

If we take the biblical numbers at face value, at least two or three million people crossed the sea that one evening. In Numbers 2:32, the total number of soldiers ready for battle among the Israelites was over 600,000 men. If we add women, children, and livestock, it was clearly an enormous undertaking. Some biblical historians have suggested that in order to accommodate such a large number, the waters of the Red Sea divided at several places along its route and that groups of Israelites crossed at various points. In any event, the division of the sea must have been extremely large for such a throng of people to pass through in a single night. The magnitude of the crowd and the extent of the preparations necessary for their survival in the desert increases when we realize the Israelites took along no long-term provisions for water and food. They had to rely on God's daily provisions. He gave them "manna" in the morning, quail in the evening, and a continuous supply of water from the rock (Ex. 16–17).

Israel in the Desert

The Desert of Sinai

After the destruction of the Egyptian army in the Red Sea, the Israelites continued their journey eastward into the wilderness of Shur. Because the word "Shur" in Hebrew means "wall," it has been suggested that this desert was located east of a wall that marked Egypt's borders at that time. In this desert Israel came to rely on God's daily provisions of manna, quail, and water. Throughout the whole of their time in the desert, God alone provided for their needs.

Moreover, God gave them victory over their enemies, such as the Amalekites (Ex. 17:8–16). According to Genesis 14:7, the territory of the Amalekites extended throughout the northern Sinai peninsula. This nation descended from Jacob's brother Esau (36:12). Presumably they attacked Israel in order to defend their territory. But they may also still have been angered over Jacob's stolen birthright and blessing (25:27–34; 27:34–35). According to Deuteronomy 25:17–19, the Amalekites attacked Israel when the latter were "weary and worn out," and they cut off their stragglers without mercy. Israel remained victorious over the Amalekites, however, as long as Moses held his hands uplifted to God. At the conclusion of the battle, the Lord commanded Moses to record the events of this battle with the people in the land for posterity (cf also Num. 21:14, where this or a similar book is called "the Book of the Wars of the LORD").

As the Israelites traversed the desert en route to the Promised Land, Moses encountered his father-in-law, Jethro (Ex. 18). Having heard of all that God had done for Israel, Jethro was anxious to meet with Moses and to learn more about those events. Apparently Jethro was a true believer in Israel's God. He even played a crucial role in instructing Moses how to administer the law to God's people.

In due time, God led Israel to Mount Sinai, also called Mount Horeb. There is considerable uncertainty about the exact location of this mountain. A long-established tradition locates the mountain near the southern tip of the Sinai peninsula, where a large, imposing range of mountains is located, with considerable room at the foot of some of them to accommodate the thousands of Israelites. Some biblical texts, however, suggest that Sinai is situated further north. In any event, we need not locate the exact site to appreciate fully the historical event, nor need we think that every individual Israelite stood precisely at the foot of the mountain. The biblical account leaves much room for picturing the Israelite camps as variously scattered throughout the region of Mount Sinai.

Covenant Forms in Israel I

When we say that God entered into a "covenant" relationship with Israel, we mean that God initiated a form of agreement that originated in the legal customs of the ancient world. When ancient covenant treaties are compared with the covenant relationship between God and Israel recounted in the Bible, we see remarkable similarities. Such treaties are characteristic of the mid–second millennium B.C., precisely when Israel stood before God at Mount Sinai.

Ancient covenant treaty documents, particularly those of Israel's neighbors (such as the Hittites), are called "suzerainty treaties," because they represent the relationship between a sovereign king (suzerain) and a loyal subject (vassal). The primary purpose of the suzerainty treaty was to establish a firm relationship of mutual support between the suzerain and his vassal. In this type of treaty, the subordinate party, the vassal, was bound by an oath to the sovereign king. The vassal was, moreover, required to obey certain stipulations that ensured his loyalty—stipulations binding only on the vassal. The suzerain on his part promised to help the vassal in time of need, but he was under no legal obligation to do so. The following elements were characteristic of this ancient covenant-treaty form:

(1) Preamble: Formal introduction identifying the author of the treaty, the suzerain.
(2) Historical prologue: A section describing, in detail, the previous relationship between the suzerain and vassal, with emphasis on the suzerain's benevolent deeds in the past.
(3) Stipulations: Specific obligations of the vassal, to ensure their absolute loyalty.
(4) Provision for the deposit of the covenant-treaty document in a central sanctuary and for its periodic public reading.
(5) List of witnesses.
(6) Curses and blessings: Served as a warning against breaking the stipulations.
(7) Formal oath ceremony: Accompanied the vassal's sworn oath of obedience.

Covenant Forms in Israel II

The Mosaic covenant shows important similarities to the type of treaties used by the Hittites with their vassals. This is not to say that God used a "Hittite treaty" to establish his relationship with Israel. It is only to say that certain features of the covenant treaties of the ancient world lent themselves to the full expression of Yahweh's relationship to Israel. These features are shared by the Hittite treaties because they were apparently common in international relations during the second millennium B.C.

Not only is the covenant form noticeable in Exodus 19–24, it can also be seen in the book of Deuteronomy; in fact, the structure of the entire book itself appears to follow the "covenant treaty" form. Since part of the stipulation of the covenant treaty was the periodic public reading of the treaty document, these documents were frequently updated or "renewed" in a formal ceremony. Many features of Deuteronomy suggest that it may have been written as a document for precisely such an occasion.

(1) Preamble (Deut. 1:1–5)
(2) Historical prologue (Deut 1:6–4:49)
(3) Two large stipulation sections are found in chapters 5–26:
  (a) Chapters 5–11 present the covenant way of life in more general and comprehensive terms.
  (b) Chapters 12–26 add more specific requirements to the covenant way of life.
(4) Curses and blessings (chs. 27–30)
(5) Provisions of continual maintenance of the covenant (chs. 31–34)
  Included in this section are two elements of the vassal treaty form:
  (a) Calling of witnesses to attest to the covenant (chs. 32–33).
  (b) Provision for public reading of the covenant (31:9–13)

Wandering in the Desert

Much of Israel's wandering in the desert is passed over in the biblical narrative itself, though a few things are recorded by later prophets, such as Amos (5:26) and Ezekiel (Ezek. 20).

The cause of Israel's wandering is explained in detail. In preparation for entering the land of Canaan, God instructed Moses to send spies from each tribe into the land (Num. 13:2). They were to report on the productivity of the land and its military strength. After spending forty days in the land, the spies returned to Moses at Kadesh with their report. Though they raved about the abundant produce of the land, they gave a fearful report of its inhabitants. The cities appeared invincible and their armies were composed of giants. Only two of the twelve spies, Joshua and Caleb, encouraged Israel to take the land. The rest advised against it.

Consequently, Israel refused at this time to obey God's order to take the land. Because of their unfaithfulness they were sentenced to remain in the desert for the rest of their lives, and their sons and daughters would inherit the land. After an abortive attempt to take the land without God's help, the people of Israel resigned themselves to God's judgment and settled down in the desert, living for the most part around the area of Kadesh Barnea.

Had it not been for Moses, the Lord might well have destroyed all the people of Israel then and there, beginning a new people from the descendants of Moses (cf. Num. 14:12). Moses, however, in response to God's intent, argued that the rejection of Israel at such a crucial moment would have a lasting effect on the nations all around who had heard of what the Lord had done in Egypt (14:13–19). As a result, the Lord was gracious to the Israelites and pardoned them. But the entire generation of those Israelites who had not trusted God and obeyed his command to take the land died in the desert, unable to see and possess the land of Canaan (14:29).

Apparently many Israelites during their time in the desert grew increasingly distant from the Lord. Though the biblical historian does not mention it, later prophets allude to the fact that many forsook God altogether during this period and followed after the gods of their Canaanite neighbors. Amos, for example, suggests that Israel as a whole ceased to offer sacrifices to God and worshiped instead at the shrine of other gods (Amos 5:26). Ezekiel claims that "their hearts were devoted to their idols" (Ezek. 20:16) and that they "lusted after their fathers' idols" (20:24).

Some, such as Joshua, did remain faithful and followed Moses' leadership. Moreover, the new generation whom Moses addressed in his last days appears to have remained faithful.

Balaam

The account of Balaam (Num. 22–24) raises a series of historical questions. When the Israelites reached the plains of Moab in the Transjordan region, their presence alarmed the local residents. Balak, the king of Moab, took counsel with the elders of the Midianites and sent for Balaam to curse the Israelites. It was the custom in the ancient Near East to perform magical curses of one's enemies as a way of assuring victory in battle. Balaam, who lived far away in Mesopotamia, apparently had a wide reputation as one who was able to pronounce such curses. According to Joshua 13:22, he was a "diviner," that is, one who was able to foretell future events. Such persons were, in fact, "an abomination to the LORD" (Deut. 18:10–13).

When Balaam came to curse Israel, he found that he could only bless them instead. Though he wanted to do otherwise, the Lord was sovereign over him and permitted him only to speak words of blessing (Num. 23:5, 12, 16). Throughout the biblical account of the nation of Israel, one basic idea recurs: The Lord blesses his people in spite of all that the nations do or say. In his wisdom, even the attempts of the nations to curse Israel are turned into occasions for their blessing. In the final analysis, however, Balaam turned against Israel and counseled the Midianites in a scheme to betray them.

In the history of biblical studies, Balaam has created much division of opinion. Early Greek and Latin church fathers regarded him essentially as a pagan magician who was brought into God's service against his own will. Others viewed him as a true prophet of sorts, but who fell from grace because of his own greed. Neither assessment tells the whole story. It is true that Balaam was a diviner and that he was paid with a "diviner's fee" (Num. 22:7). But it is also true that he did have a previous relationship to the Lord and a direct knowledge of him. In 22:8, Balaam sought the Lord's will as to whether or not he should go with Balak's messengers, and he received an answer from the Lord.

Throughout the story, Balaam is portrayed as a spokesman for God. God even foretells the future of the nation of Israel through him—events that would be realized both in the days of Saul and David and in the far distant days of the Messiah. How, then, are we to understand this unique character Balaam? Though Balaam was a pagan diviner, he apparently came across elements of the true knowledge of Israel's God, either through tradition or through reports of the great things God had done for Israel in Egypt. In that way, Balaam was drawn to identify himself with the Lord without, however, actually becoming a prophet.

The Conquest and the Judges

The Conquest of the Land of Canaan

As punishment for their refusal to trust God (Num. 14), the generation of Israelites who came out of Egypt was sentenced to die in the desert. They could not enjoy God's blessing of the land. Moses, because of a similar lack of faith (Num. 20), was also not permitted to lead the new generation of Israelites into the land. That task was given to Joshua, who had led the armies of Israel in their first victory over the Amalekites (Ex. 17).

The first stage of the conquest came while Moses was still alive and in command of Israel's armies. He sent messengers to the king of Edom, requesting permission to pass through their territory en route to the land of Canaan. That request, however, was flatly rejected. Hence Israel was forced to go south around their territory and enter the border regions of Canaan through Moab and Ammon. After several significant victories in these border regions east of the Jordan River (cf. Num. 21; Deut. 1–3), Moses commissioned Joshua as his successor. Shortly after that Moses died and was buried—near the border of the land, but outside its boundaries. Israel had gained control of virtually all the regions east of the Jordan.

After the death of Moses, Israel moved quickly into the land of Canaan west of the Jordan by attacking the border town of Jericho. Through a miraculous stratagem, the walls of the city collapsed before Joshua's army, and its inhabitants were delivered into their hands. The conquest of Canaan proceeded through a series of successful and strategically important battles. Joshua's armies were seemingly invincible. In what appears to be record time, the entire land was captured and placed under Israelite rule. We learn after the death of Joshua, however, that his victories were short-lived. Much remained in conquering the land for the future generations.

After taking Jericho, Joshua's conquest of Canaan centered on three geographical regions: the central hill country, the northern plains, and the southern desert. Their campaign for the central hill country actually began with the capture of Jericho. The next stage of the campaign proved disastrous. Because one Israelite had disobeyed God and taken part of the spoils of war for his own use, their initial attempts to capture the small outpost called Ai failed. But God gave them further victories over the entire central region. Joshua and his forces then turned southward. Hearing of their success, a coalition of southern city-states was hastily formed to defend that region, but to no avail. Joshua's army defeated that coalition and subdued the southern territory. A similar coalition formed in the far north, but they also were defeated and their cities captured.

Settlement of the Land

The remaining years of Joshua's leadership were spent parceling out the land among the twelve tribes of Israel. Territories within each parcel remained to be settled by each individual tribe. As a final gesture in uniting the people, Joshua called all the leaders together at the centrally located city of Shechem, and there he renewed God's covenant with them.

After Joshua's death, each tribe set out to occupy its own allotted territory. The biblical historian focuses his attention on the exploits of the tribe of Judah, the central tribe from the point of view of the royal house of David. For the most part, Judah was successful in taking possession of their territory. The Bible emphasizes that it was the Lord alone who gave them victory over the Canaanites. Among their many successful conquests, they captured Jerusalem and set it on fire. But they did not settle in the city at that time. Instead, they went on to occupy their allotment in the southern hill country, where God continued to give them a great victory.

The tribe of Judah, however, was not as successful in the lower coastal plains of their territory, perhaps because those regions were defended by iron chariots (cf. Judg. 1:19). Strictly speaking, the biblical historian does not say Judah was "unable" to possess the plains territory, only that they "did not" possess it. That phrase leaves open more than one reason for God's not allowing them to possess those cities. Some have supposed, for example, that God allowed the Canaanites to remain in those cities with their iron chariots in order that they might be a means of "testing" Israel in the ways of war (3:1).

Though Judah had burned part of Jerusalem (Judg. 1:8), enough of it remained to mount a partially successful defense against a further attack by the Benjaminites (1:21). Its inhabitants at that time were called the Jebusites. Apparently the Benjamites were able to gain a foothold in the city and thus lived there along with the Jebusites for a considerable period of time. Jerusalem was located along the border of the allotments of the tribes of Judah and Benjamin. Both tribes, in fact, were allotted the city by Joshua (Josh. 15:8, 63; 18:16, 28). The city was not completely taken from the Jebusites until the reign of King David (2 Sam. 5:6).

The remaining tribes appear to have had nominal success in occupying their territories. The biblical writer notes a whole series of battles, but, for the most part, these battles ended inconclusively, with the Israelites living alongside the Canaanites within each of the tribal territories. That lack of success went hand in hand with a serious religious and moral decline in Israel. The true worship of God appears to have almost died out (cf. Judg. 2:20).

The Office of the Judge in Ancient Israel

Early Israel was a tribal federation united around a common worship of God. From its earliest days the concept of a kingdom predominated, though an actual monarchy was not established until much later. Behind the administration of everyday affairs was a *theocracy*—God was the true King in Israel. His rule, however, was carried out by divinely selected individuals and institutions. Moses, Israel's first political and religious leader, was both a king (Deut. 33:5) and a prophet (18:15). He also founded the official priesthood, the house of Aaron. In this single individual, all the central institutions of government were embodied.

After Moses' death, his central position was divided up among several other individuals or institutions. Joshua assumed the military and political leadership of the tribes. The priesthood continued through the descendants of the house of Aaron. Their close associates, the Levites, performed the bulk of the religious duties as they had been assigned by Moses. Then there were prophets, who spoke to the people and their leaders on God's behalf. And the judges taught the people God's law and helped them apply it to everyday life. The office of judge had been established by Moses as the central office for each Israelite town or city (Deut. 16:18); a higher court of appeal was located at the site of the tabernacle (17:8ff.), which heard cases too difficult for the local judges.

After the death of Joshua and the elders who served Israel with him, the nation plunged into deep apostasy. For the concept of a theocracy to continue in Israel, divine intervention was necessary. To save the nation from ruin, God raised up a succession of select warriors and courageous women to serve as judges and to save the people from the oppression of their enemies. Empowered by God's Spirit, these individuals rallied the nation, united the tribes, and booted their enemies out of the land.

Our image of the judges is dominated by figures such as Gideon, Deborah, and Samson. But there was another side to their mission. Once the enemy had been dealt a fatal blow, the people had to be led back to God and his word. Much of their ministry was devoted to the study and teaching of that word throughout the land. As such, these early leaders became the prototype, the model, of what God ultimately desired of the king. One of the great shortcomings of the first king, Saul, is that, though a great military leader, he failed to lead the people into obedience of God's word. Perhaps David's greatest achievement, on the other hand, was his being both a courageous military leader and a man after God's own heart. David knew the importance of both political power and godly leadership. God was his true leader, and Israel's.

The Activities of the Judges

The book of Judges is our primary source for understanding the activities of the judges during Israel's early history. It presents a highly stylized version of their activity. The author is primarily interested in making a theological point and thus selected his material carefully. Fortunately, to fill out his picture of this era, the author has appended several vivid pictures of what everyday life was like during this time (Judg. 17–21). We also have the book of Ruth as another perspective on this period. While Judges presents a bleak view of the ungodly conditions during most of this period, Ruth gives us a glimpse of the faithful remnant of God's people.

Judges introduces us to the lives and activities of twelve Israelite judges.

(1) Othniel (3:7–11): As judgment for their apostasy, God delivered Israel into the hands of the Aramean king Cushan-Rishathaim. When they called out to him in repentance, God raised up Othniel to drive the Arameans out of the land. He then "judged" the people for the next forty years—that is, he taught them to live according to God's word.

(2) Ehud (3:12–30): Ehud delivered Israel from the oppression of the Moabite king Eglon. Ehud used his own unique physical limitations, "a restricted right hand," to carry out his divinely appointed task—he dealt an unexpected fatal blow to the king with his left hand.

(3) Shamgar (3:31): Shamgar killed six hundred Philistines with an ox-goad.

(4) Deborah (4:1–5:31): As judge of Israel, Deborah rallied the reluctant warrior Barak to drive back the Canaanites in the north. God used a courageous and resourceful woman, Jael, to kill the Canaanite warrior Sisera.

(5) Gideon (6:1–8:35): Gideon delivered Israel from oppression by the Midianites.

(6) Tola (10:1–2): Tola saved Israel from their oppressors and judged twenty-three years.

(7) Jair (10:3–5): Jair was a wealthy man who judged Israel twenty-two years.

(8) Jephthah (10:6–12:7): Jephthah rose from an ignoble beginning to become judge over all Israel, defeating the Ammonites.

(9) Ibzan (12:8–10): Ibzan, from Bethlehem, was a judge in Israel for seven years.

(10) Elon (12:11–13): Elon, from Zebulun, judged Israel ten years.

(11) Abdon (12:14–15): Abdon, from Ephraim, judged Israel eight years.

(12) Samson (13:1–16:31): One of the most unusual judges, Samson began the drive to rid Israel of the Philistine threat. He is noted for his wholehearted zeal for the people of God.

Samuel, the Last of the Judges

Samuel was the last of the judges who ruled Israel before the time of the monarchy. He was personally dedicated to God before he was born (1 Sam. 1:11). During his early years, Israel faced some of its darkest days. The ark of the covenant was captured and profaned by the Philistines, and Israel was overrun by their enemies. But Samuel was able to rally the Israelites to renew their trust in the Lord and to deliver them from the Philistines (17:3–13).

At the end of Samuel's life, after many years as judge, a crisis in leadership developed over the kind of leader Israel was to have in the future. Samuel, knowing that his days as judge in Israel were limited, appointed his two sons to succeed him in that office. But these sons abused their office, and the people were not willing to let them continue. They thus came to Samuel with the request to appoint a king, "such as all the other nations have" (1 Sam. 8:4–5). Samuel strongly objected to this request, seeing it as a rejection of his own rule. God, however, stepped into the picture, telling Samuel to grant the request of the people and appoint a king. Samuel heeded God's word and, reluctantly, appointed Saul as king over Israel.

In giving in to the people's request, Samuel issued a stern warning to the Israelites to remain faithful to the original covenant in which the Lord, and he alone, was truly their king (1 Sam. 8:11–22; 12:14–15). The seeming hesitation on the part of God to provide Israel with a king is puzzling to some in view of the overall importance the kingship was to have throughout Israel's history. It must be noted, however, that the institution of kingship was already established at the time of Moses (Deut. 17:14), when God gave specific instructions regarding the kind of king Israel was to have—someone who knew him, obeyed his word, and led the people in their obedience to God's word. But this type of king was not on the mind of the people when they requested a king. They were patterning themselves after the other nations, looking for a great military leader, whereas God desired a great spiritual leader for his people.

It is significant that the king they received, Saul, was much what they desired. He gathered a great army about him (1 Sam. 10:26) and proved courageous in battle (11:11). But in the area of spiritual leadership Saul fell short of God's requirement, for he failed to keep God's commands (13:13–14). Samuel's displeasure over Israel's desire for a king stemmed from his misunderstanding of the motives of the people. Israel was not rejecting him as leader. Rather, they were rejecting the kind of leadership God intended them to have. They wanted to choose their own king, whereas God wanted to choose for them the king they should have.

The United Monarchy

Saul's Monarchy

Saul's name, which means "the one asked for," epitomized the role he was to play in biblical history. He was the king the people asked for to replace the judges. Saul was a member of the tribe of Benjamin. Not only could little good be said about that tribe from the book of Judges, but also this was not that tribe who was ultimately to provide the royal lineage in Israel.

Saul had all the external qualifications of a great leader. He was physically strong and a great warrior. An important part of his commission was to deliver Israel from the hands of the Philistines (1 Sam. 9:16). He immediately set out to accomplish that task and enjoyed considerable success (14:15–23). But Saul had some traits that rendered him unfit to serve as Israel's king.

Primarily he failed to show spiritual leadership. A critical moment came when the Philistines had gathered with 30,000 chariots and 6,000 horsemen to war with Saul and his armies (1 Sam. 13:5). The ranks of Saul's armies began to abandon their positions when they saw the impending Philistine threat (13:8). Saul had been told by Samuel to wait until he came in seven days and that he, Samuel, would offer a sacrifice before engaging the Philistines in battle. To Saul's credit he waited six days. But, on the seventh day, when Samuel still had not arrived, Saul disobeyed the word of Samuel and offered the sacrifice himself, thus breaking a fundamental stipulation of the king within Israel's theocratic rule: The king was, at all times, to obey the word of God's prophet. In refusing to wait, Saul rejected not only the authority of the prophet, but, more importantly, the authority of the Lord, the true King in Israel. It was, in fact, considered by God as a foolish act of rebellion, and for it, Saul lost his kingship.

The Bible records a second occasion on which Saul revealed that he was ill-suited for the theocratic kingship. When commanded by Samuel to "totally destroy" all that belonged to the Amalekites as an act of divine judgment against them (1 Sam. 15:1–3), Saul relented and saved some of the spoils of war for himself (15:9). When Samuel heard of Saul's failure to carry out God's word, he pronounced the end of Saul's kingship and began seeking a replacement. That process was to culminate in the anointing of David, from the tribe of Judah, as king.

The last years of Saul's life were marked by an increasing failure to lead God's people in obedience to God's word. He experienced a fierce rivalry with David. He spent much of his time trying to hunt down David in order to kill him. Ultimately he took his own life during a humiliating defeat by the Philistines—the very people he had been commissioned to suppress.

David's Rise to the Throne

David, the youngest son of Jesse, of the tribe of Judah, was the second and most successful king in Israel. Under him, the Israelite kingdom reached its pinnacle, both politically and spiritually. The kingdom he established outlasted all others in Israel. At the time of the Babylonian exile, there were still descendants of David on the throne.

The biblical writers were interested in the early history of this family. It begins with Judah and Tamar in Genesis 38 and continues through Boaz and Ruth in the book of Ruth. David came from a godly line in Israel, one marked by faithfulness and trust in the Lord. When God rejected Saul as king, he immediately sent the prophet Samuel to the house of Jesse in order to find a king who was pleasing to God (1 Sam. 13:14). Jesse had several sons, but only David proved satisfactory to the Lord. Samuel found him tending his father's flocks, too young to be taken seriously as Israel's next king. David was immediately anointed by Samuel and received a special endowment of God's Spirit to carry out his role as king successfully (16:13).

David had to wait a long time before ascending the throne. He was thirty years old when he became king. During his time of waiting, David attempted to live peacefully with Saul, but to little avail. Much of his time was spent dodging personal threats and assaults against him by the jealous Saul. Ironically, David's first role in the company of Saul was playing a harp to comfort Saul during his fits of rage.

As a young boy, David challenged the Philistine giant Goliath. In ancient conflicts, major battles were often preceded by savage contests between mighty warriors. The outcome of the contests usually determined the outcome of the battle. Using a simple slingshot, David defeated Goliath, and the enemy was quickly routed. David demonstrated that God's kingdom could not be defended by mere spears and swords (1 Sam. 17:47). God alone would deliver Israel from the hands of their enemies.

David assumed the throne as king over Judah immediately after the death of Saul (2 Sam. 2). The biblical narratives give two accounts of Saul's death. In the one, Saul dies in his last battle with the Philistines by falling on his own sword (1 Sam. 31). That appears to be the true account. In the second account, told by an escaping Amalekite, Saul lived for some time after falling on his sword and was slain by the Amalekite (2 Sam. 1). David took no chance of letting the Amalekite go unpunished for lifting his hand against the Lord's anointed. Following closely after Saul's death was the murder of Saul's general, Abner. Though David was innocent in the matter, the removal of Abner led directly to David's acceptance as king by the nation as a whole.

David's Reign Over Israel

Immediately preceding David's rise to the throne, Israel had been divided into two separate kingdoms. David began by ruling only Judah, whereas Saul's son Ish-Bosheth ruled what remained of Saul's kingdom in the north. Politically, that region was called Israel. But after Ish-Bosheth's death, David ruled all Israel. The kingdoms of David and Solomon thus represent a unique period in Israel's history when the entire nation was united under a single king.

A significant feature of David's united kingdom was his establishment of the centrally located city of Jerusalem as his capital. Up to then, neither the tribe of Judah nor Benjamin had been able to capture the city permanently. Once his kingdom was secured and his enemies subdued, David set out to unite further the nation by building a permanent dwelling place for God, the temple. Following closely the plans laid out by Moses for building the tabernacle in the desert, David gathered materials and workers to construct a temple in Jerusalem. Only divine intervention prohibited him from fulfilling these plans. That task was to await his son, Solomon.

As a reward for David's faithfulness to the Lord, God made a special covenant with the dynasty of David, in which he promised that a "descendant" of the house of David would establish an eternal kingdom in Jerusalem. That Davidic descendant would be a faithful king like David himself. Solomon apparently understood his own reign to be a fulfillment of God's covenant promise. The biblical writers are clear, however, that neither Solomon nor any of the subsequent Davidic kings could be reckoned as the true fulfillment (1 Kings 11:9–13). Thus the promise made to David went beyond any of the Davidic kings. It pointed to a future messianic king who would establish God's kingdom in Jerusalem forever. That promise finds its fulfillment in the reign of Jesus, the Son of David.

Though David's reign prefigured the reign of the future Messiah, David's own life had many shortcomings and ultimately ended in disgrace. At the height of his reign, he committed an act of adultery with Bathsheba, the wife of Uriah, one of his trusted warriors. To cover his deed, David ordered that Uriah be killed in battle (2 Sam. 11). David had the courage to confess his wrong and seek God's forgiveness, but the effect of his disobedience was felt throughout his kingdom for many generations. In his own lifetime, one of his most beloved sons, Absalom, mounted a full-scale rebellion against David. He himself seems to have lost some of his confidence in God's protection towards the end of his life. In the end, however, David's trust in God's promises remained firm, and he died in the hope of a future glorious kingdom.

The Building of Solomon's Monarchy

The last days of David's reign were marked by a dispute over his successor. Since Absalom, his oldest son, was dead, his next oldest, Adonijah, made public preparation to assume the kingship. His plans evidently met with agreement among the members of David's court. But those plans did not sit well with everyone. David's wife, Bathsheba, Zadok the priest, Nathan the prophet, and others close to David made counter plans to make Solomon king. While Adonijah and his followers were celebrating, Solomon was quickly escorted to the Spring of Gihon, where he was anointed king by the priest Zadok.

After David died, Adonijah, who had been pardoned by Solomon, made another attempt to gain the throne but failed. He was executed, and Abiathar, his priest, was replaced by Zadok. Joab, the faithful general of David's army, who had supported Adonijah, was also executed.

Solomon's task was clearly cut out for him. He had to administer the kingdom built by David. Recognizing the scope of that task, one of his first acts was to pray for divine wisdom to rule the people of Israel (1 Kings 3:9).

Solomon sought to maintain good relationships with the foreign rulers around him through a system of trade alliances, many of which were sealed, as was customary in the ancient world, by marriage. Thus many foreign women entered Solomon's household. Rehoboam, Solomon's successor, was the offspring of such a union (1 Kings 14:21). Solomon's most distinguished wife was the daughter of the Egyptian pharaoh. His most important trade alliance was with the region of Tyre, a Phoenician stronghold headed by Hiram. This alliance was an important means for securing materials for building the temple. But Solomon's policy was detrimental to the spiritual vitality of the nation. It led to Israel's forsaking the Lord and following other gods.

Solomon experienced considerable difficulties along two fronts. In the south, the Edomite prince Hadad joined an alliance with Egypt against Solomon. He led a series of unsuccessful but troublesome revolts against Solomon's rule in Edom. In the north, the Aramaic general Rezon wrestled control of Damascus and became a major adversary of Solomon.

One of Solomon's greatest achievements lay in the area of international trade. He made full use of Israel's geographic location along the great trade routes of the ancient world. Solomon amassed a fleet of merchant ships in his southern port cities, manned by Phoenician sailors, which carried on lucrative trade with distant parts of Africa. He also maintained an overland caravan route to Arabia and traded in horses and chariots as far away as the cities of Asia Minor.

The Administration of Solomon's Monarchy

Solomon greatly strengthened the economic conditions of his father's kingdom through his policies with foreign nations. But the real greatness of his reign consisted of his domestic policies, which brought integral strength and stability to his kingdom. His wise trade relationships greatly increased his own personal wealth and the wealth of many within his kingdom. Archaeological evidence suggests that the centers of his government, both the city of Jerusalem and other cities, greatly expanded during his reign. Improvements and inventions in the agriculture techniques of the day also aided the productivity of his farmers and resulted in increased food supplies to his cities.

Solomon developed an elaborate civil and military administration. He divided his kingdom into twelve administrative regions (1 Kings 4:7–19) and subjected many of their residents to forced labor in order to accommodate the material demands of his growing kingdom. Solomon also established heavily fortified cities to accommodate his growing military presence among the people (9:15–19). His rule began to take on the appearance of a medieval fuedal lord. He amassed 1,400 chariots and 12,000 horsemen and garrisoned them in "chariot cities" throughout his kingdom (10:26). Such cities, linked to storage cities and military fortifications, were designed to protect Solomon's extensive trade routes.

Solomon's reign was also a time of great cultural advances. The nation experienced a high rate of literacy. Various groups fostered learning, and culture flourished, producing much of the literary material now found in the Bible (including especially the book of Proverbs). Solomon himself was internationally known for his literary skill and insight (1 Kings 5:10–14).

Solomon's administrative court maintained official records that later served as source material for the biblical historical narratives (1 Kings 11:41). Books such as Joshua, Judges, and Samuel may have been composed during his reign. Many of the psalms of David were collected to form early editions of the Psalter (cf. Ps. 72:20). Moreover, musical instruments were produced from exotic imported woods, and new psalms were written (cf. Ps. 127).

From the standpoint of the biblical writers, Solomon's greatest accomplishment was his construction of the temple in Jerusalem. Though David had already laid the plans for the temple, Solomon supervised the project through to its completion. Using materials and skilled labor supplied mostly by his Phoenician neighbors, he spared no effort or expense to build a house for the God of Israel that could be rivaled by no one in the ancient world.

The Divided Kingdoms:
Israel and Judah

The Division of the Kingdom

God had made a covenant with David (2 Sam. 7:16), in which he promised that David's kingdom would endure forever and that an unbroken succession of sons, beginning with Solomon, would rule after him. Implicit in God's promise was a messianic promise of an eternal Davidic kingship.

There were, however, occasions when the legitimacy of the house of David was challenged. Already during Solomon's reign rebellion broke out in the land, spearheaded by Jeroboam, the son of Nebat, from the tribe of Ephraim (1 Kings 11:26). Being an Ephraimite, Jeroboam could lay claim to tribal privileges that reached back into the most ancient traditions. The tribe of Ephraim was of the house of Joseph, which had been blessed by God (Gen. 48:15–20; 49:22–26) and was promised a seed that would become a "group of nations" (48:19). Both Joshua and Gideon were from the house of Joseph. During the process of restoring the city of Jerusalem, Solomon noted Jeroboam's leadership ability and appointed him over the house of Joseph. At about the same time, Jeroboam was confronted by the prophet Ahijah (1 Kings 11:29), who told him that the Lord had chosen him as king of the ten northern tribes. Those tribes were to be taken away from Solomon's kingdom (11:31), though God would preserve for the house of David one tribe (11:32). That tribe was apparently the tribe of Benjamin, which the Lord preserved for David's tribe, Judah.

Solomon responded to Jeroboam's rebellion by seeking to kill him. Jeroboam fled to Egypt and found refuge with the Egyptian king Shishak until Solomon's death. Historians believe Shishak gave asylum to Solomon's enemy because he hoped one day to regain Egyptian control over that part of his kingdom.

After Solomon's death, the ten northern tribes initially recognized Rehoboam, Solomon's son, as his successor, but they insisted he lighten the load that Solomon had imposed on them (1 Kings 12:4). Foolishly, Rehoboam refused to listen and was thus rejected by the northern tribes (12:15–16). The result was the division of the kingdom. Jeroboam returned from exile and was made king, and Rehoboam ruled only over the tribes of Judah and Benjamin (12: 20–21). There were serious spiritual consequences to the loss of the Davidic kingdom. Jerusalem, the place where God was to be worshiped, was no longer accessible to all the people of Israel. Jeroboam, the king of the northern tribes of Israel, built two new worship sites within the boundaries of his kingdom—one at Bethel, along the southern border, and the other at Dan, along his northern border. Jeroboam also established a new priesthood and set up idols.

Rehoboam

Not only were the spiritual consequences of the division of David's kingdom great, so were the political and economic consequences. The Aramean states to the north of David's kingdom were able to develop on their own into a formidable force. Within a short period of time they became a serious threat to both Israel in the north and Judah in the south. Moreover, Ammon and Moab, to the east of both the kingdoms, gained their independence and posed a serious threat. Such a shift in the balance of power in the region affected trade relations and thus had a serious impact on the overall economic security of both Israel and Judah.

The Bible gives few specific details about the reign of Rehoboam. During his lifetime Judah fell into grievous sins (1 Kings 14:22–24), for the king established "high places, sacred stones and Asherah poles on every high hill and under every spreading tree." These were signs of false worship. "High places" were mounds of stone where altars were set up for worship; they were commonly used in Canaanite worship. "Sacred stones" and "Asherah poles" are associated in the Bible with the high places. The "sacred stone" was a stone pillar erected to represent a deity; it was not a image or idol as such, but a symbol of a god. The "Asherah pole" was a wooden post or stake that represented a female deity at the high places. At times these poles were identified with special trees planted at or near a sacred site. The Bible frequently refers to these high places as situated in the shade of a grove of flourishing green trees.

The Bible does not tell us to what extent the Israelites took over the Canaanite religious beliefs and practices during their periods of great sin and apostasy. However, it is clear that the high places and all that went with them angered God. In times of revival they were torn down and destroyed (2 Kings 18:4; 23:1–15). Israel's prophets frequently railed against these high places (Jer. 7:31; Hos. 10:8; Amos 7:9). The writer of the book of Kings condemns every king in Israel and Judah, except Hezekiah and Josiah, for not destroying the high places.

Also during Rehoboam's reign over Judah, the kingdom was invaded and decimated by the Egyptian king Shishak (1 Kings 14:25). This was an act of divine judgment. Shishak, a Libyan, had come to power in Egypt in 945 B.C. and was anxious to extend Egypt's rule again into Palestine. We know from archaeological remains of his battles as well as Shishak's own inscription that he wreaked havoc on Israel and Judah. Many of the strong fortifications that Rehoboam had built in Judah (2 Chron. 11:5–12) were destroyed at this time. Once Shishak had decimated the two kingdoms, he had to return to solve problems of his own in Egypt.

Jeroboam

When he broke away from the Davidic kingdom in Judah, Jeroboam was afraid that his subjects would reassert their previous loyalties to the house of David if they continued to worship God in Jerusalem, the city God had ordained as the throne of his eternal kingdom. To prevent his subjects from going annually to Jerusalem, Jeroboam built two centers of worship within his own borders—one at Bethel in the south, the other at Dan in the far north. This was a grievous sin (1 Kings 12:30), for it violated the central tenet of Israel's covenant with God and exposed the people to the dangers of idolatry. As if to increase that danger, Jeroboam set up two golden calves (12:28), apparently in imitation of the one fashioned by Aaron in the Sinai desert (Ex. 32:4)—surely a blatant affront to the law of Moses.

What motivated Jeroboam to carry out such a disastrous scheme? Perhaps Jeroboam was attempting to unite a wide variety of beliefs in his realm, including some of the Canaanite people. Or perhaps Jeroboam did not intend the images to be worshiped, but only to represent the throne or pedestal of God. The book of Kings, however, clearly identifies these golden calves as "idols" (1 Kings 14:9). Jeroboam himself says of the calves, "Here are your gods ... who brought you up out of Egypt" (12:28). Whatever his intentions, Jeroboam clearly established a rival worship in the north that was acceptable to the people of his realm (12:30).

God did not leave Jeroboam's actions unchallenged, however. He sent a "man of God" from Judah to proclaim words of judgment against Jeroboam and his kingdom, who visited the king during a special feast day at Bethel. The title "man of God" was one of honor, usually identifying a prophet of God. This prophet's mission was to confront Jeroboam openly with his sin of initiating false worship in Israel. The prophet also foretold of the downfall of the northern kingdom. As he was speaking to Jeroboam, the altar at which the king was standing split apart. This was taken as a sign that the prophet had truly been sent by God.

This biblical account outlines the essential role the prophets played in Israel's history: to confront a king when he strayed from God's law. The words of this prophet also point to the ultimate victory the house of David was to have over the northern kingdom, when the Davidic king Josiah destroyed the false worship centers at Bethel and Dan (cf. 2 Kings 23:16). Later God sent another prophet to King Jeroboam to announce that his kingdom would be taken away from him. Thus the northern kingdom of Israel did not receive divine sanction from the words of the prophets. God's promise to David remained linked to David's future Son.

The Successors to Jeroboam in the North

The political climate of the northern kingdom of Israel from 901 to 876 B.C. was characterized by instability and dynastic change. Nadab, Jeroboam's son, reigned as king only two years (901–900 B.C.). He was killed in a coup by Baasha (1 Kings 15:27), a warrior from the tribe of Isaachar. This man held the throne from 900–877 B.C., but his son Elah reigned only two years (877–876 B.C.). He was killed in a plot hatched by one of his military commanders, Zimri. But Zimri reigned only one week, having not been able to rally sufficient support around him from the general populace. Omri, another of Elah's military commanders, who had a much larger base of public support, attacked Zimri in the capital city Tirzah and killed him (876 B.C.).

Omni reigned for a relatively long period of time, after subduing other contenders to the throne (876–869 B.C.). The biblical authors devote little attention to Omri, even though, politically speaking, he was one of Israel's most important kings. Omri turned the unpredictable political affairs of the northern kingdom into a relatively stable and long-lived dynasty. Long after his dynasty had died out, the northern kingdom was known to its Assyrian neighbors as "the house of Omri."

During this period Israel enjoyed a great deal of material prosperity. A new capital was built in Samaria, with a great palace and military fortifications. Some of those buildings remain today. Similar constructions were carried out throughout the northern kingdom. The walls of major cities were strengthened or rebuilt, along with the digging of water tunnels for use during times of siege.

Though usually regarded as politically shrewd and opportunistic, in general the kings of Omri's dynasty contributed much to the general decline of spiritual vitality in the northern kingdom. These kings, such as King Ahab, became central archetypes of the oppression of the poor and godly remnants of God's people in Israel (cf. 1 Kings 21). In order to strengthen their overall political position in the ancient world, they engaged in numerous alliances with foreign nations. The infamous marriage of King Ahab with the Phoenician queen Jezebel was probably the result of one such alliance. It was to Israel's advantage to be allied with the Phoenicians during Ahab's reign because Phoenicia was at the height of its power and had greatly increased its wealth through extensive colonialization and trade.

Israel's northern neighbors during the dynasty of Omri, the Arameans, were a powerful and aggressive people, led by Ben-Hadad, the king of Damascus. Ben-Hadad besieged Israel in Samaria during Ahab's reign (1 Kings 20:1ff.), but they were defeated. Ben-Hadad then launched a second attack on Samaria at the end of that same year (1 Kings 20:26), but he was again defeated. A period of three years of peace followed, at the end of which Ahab joined Jehoshaphat of Judah in waging a brief war with the Arameans. In the ensuing battle Ahab was killed (1 Kings 22:37). Though not mentioned in the Bible, ancient records show that Ahab, on at least one occasion, was an ally with the Arameans against the rising threat of the Assyrians. In 859 B.C., Shalmaneser III invaded the Aramean regions of Syria, reaching as far as the Mediterranean Sea. Israel under Ahab joined with the Aramean city-states and fought an indecisive battle in 853 B.C.

The Fall of the House of Ahab

Ahab was succeeded by his son Ahaziah (1 Kings 22:51–53), who continued the priests, ceremonies, and worship centers established by Jeroboam at Bethel and Dan (12:25–33). He followed the gods of Israel's neighbors and forsook the God of Israel. Like his father Ahab, Ahaziah was confronted by the prophet Elijah for his idolatry. He died from an accidental fall in his palace in Samaria. He had no heir and thus was succeeded by his younger brother, Joram (Jehoram) (2 Kings 3:1–9:26).

The Bible pictures Joram as somewhat of a reformer. He got rid of, for example, the "sacred stone of Baal" that Ahab had made. Many of the prophet Elisha's deeds were performed during his reign. In fulfillment of the word of the Lord spoken by Elijah to Ahab, his father (1 Kings 21:29), God ultimately brought judgment on the house of Ahab in the death of his son Joram. This came by the hand of Jehu (2 Kings 9:24–26), who had been specifically anointed by God as an agent of his judgment (1 Kings 19:16).

Jehu, Joram's top military commander, was the son of an otherwise unknown Israelite named Jehoshaphat, the son of Nimshi. In destroying the remainder of the house of Ahab, Jehu first killed King Joram (2 Kings 9:14–26), along with Ahaziah, the king of Judah (2 Kings 9:27–29). He then went after Jezebel, the wife of Ahab, and, with the help of the inhabitants of Jezreel, killed her (9:30–37). With her death the word of the prophet Elijah was fulfilled (9:36; cf. 1 Kings 21:23–24). Jehu then set out to eradicate the remainder of the house of Ahab, including Ahab's seventy sons in Samaria (2 Kings 10:1–10) and all who remained in Jezreel, including "his chief men, his close friends and his priests" (10:11). He traveled throughout the countryside executing any survivors (10:12–17). Jehu then turned against the priests and servants of Baal and destroyed Baal worship in Israel (10:18–29).

Though recounting these events in graphic detail, the writer of Kings takes pains to show that Jehu acted according to the Lord's will and as the instrument of divine justice against the idolatry of the nation (2 Kings 10:30). Ironically, in spite of Jehu's religious zeal, he did not remove the false worship centers of Bethel and Dan and hence continued in "the sins of Jeroboam" (10:29, 31). For this neglect, God sent Hazael of Aram against him (cf. 1 Kings 19:15b; 2 Kings 8:7–15). Hazael did not destroy the house of Jehu, but he did reduce its wealth and the size of his kingdom. Jehu lost to Hazael most of his territory east of the Jordan River. But because of his loyalty in carrying out God's judgment against the house of Ahab, Jehu was rewarded with the promise of a successful dynasty, one that would last four generations (10:30).

The House of Jehu (842–745 B.C.)

Jehu (842–815 B.C.) founded a dynasty in Israel that lasted for nearly a century. During that time, political conditions throughout the Near East were changing rapidly. The Assyrian empire was on the rise. Israel was being pulled into the affairs of those empires that were just beginning to spread their influence across her borders. By the end of the dynasty of Jehu in the mid-eighth century, Assyria could no longer be ignored.

Jehoahaz (815–801 B.C.), the son of Jehu, succeeded him to the throne (2 Kings 13:1). Like Israelite kings before him, he did not remove the high places at Bethel and Dan that Jeroboam had set up (13:2); thus, God sent Hazael king of Aram against him (13:3; cf. 8:12; 1 Kings 19:15). Jehoahaz repented, and God sent Israel a deliverer (2 Kings 13:4–5). The writer of Kings does not identify this deliverer. Perhaps Jehoash son of Jehoahaz was the deliverer in that he "recaptured from Ben-Hadad son of Hazael the towns he had taken in battle from his father Jehoahaz" (13:25). He did this because "the LORD was gracious to them and had compassion" (13:23). A similar situation occurred for much the same reason during the reign of his son, Jeroboam II (14:25–27).

Jehoash (801–786 B.C.) (2 Kings 13:10–25; 14:15–16) did not rise above the other kings of Israel. During his reign, the great prophet Elisha died. Jehoash's sorrowful response to Elisha's illness is a witness to the high regard with which he was held even by a king who did evil in God's eyes. Also during his reign, Israel was oppressed by Hazael. God was gracious and compassionate and did not let Hazael destroy the people of Israel.

Jeroboam II (786–746 B.C.), the son of Jehoash (2 Kings 14:23–29), followed in the footsteps of his namesake, Jeroboam, the son of Nebat. Jonah lived during his reign and prophesied about the restoration of Israel's eastern borders (14:25)—a prophecy fulfilled through Jeroboam II. This king also recaptured the Aramean cities of Damascus and Hamath. Hosea and Amos were contemporaries of this king and directed their prophecies to his excesses.

Zechariah (746–745 B.C.), the son of Jeroboam II, reigned for six months after succeeding his father. He was assassinated and succeeded by Shallum, the son of Jabesh. Shallum, whose lineage is not clearly established, brought the dynasty of Jehu to an end, thus fulfilling of the Lord's prophecy to Jehu that his dynasty would fall after the fourth generation (2 Kings 15:12). Shallum (15:13–16) was himself assassinated by Menahem after only one month (15:14).

The Fall of the Northern Kingdom of Israel

Israel endured the hard rule of Menahem (2 Kings 15:17–22) for ten years (746–737 B.C.). During his reign, Tiglath-Pileser III (745–727 B.C.), called Pul in 15:19, gained ascendancy as king of Assyria and marched against the weakened city states of Syria to his west. He imposed a heavy tribute on the major cities along the Mediterranean coast. Peace could now only be obtained, even in Israel, with the price of silver and the taxation of every Israelite, particularly the wealthy. We read of Menahem's plight, along with that of many other local kings and chieftains, in Tiglath-Pileser's own annals. Menaham's son, Pekahiah (737–736 B.C.) succeeded him, but he was assassinated by one of his military leaders, Pekah (736–732 B.C.).

In Pekah's day Tiglath-Pileser captured a major portion of northern Israel's land (2 Kings 15:29) and deported its people. Pekah sought an alliance with the Aramean king Rezin (740–732 B.C.) to oppose the incursions of Assyrian power. They invited the Judean king Jotham to join in their opposition, but he refused (2 Kings 15:37). After Jotham's death, Pekah and Rezin attacked Jerusalem; the new Judean king, Ahaz, appealed to Tiglath-Pileser of Assyria for help (2 Kings 16:7; cf. Isa. 7:1–8:18), which was strongly opposed by the prophet Isaiah. He insisted that God's people should put their trust in God, not the Assyrians. But King Ahaz did not heed Isaiah's warning and carried through with his plan to seek the help of Assyria.

Tiglath-Pileser III quickly responded. He attacked Damascus and killed Rezin (2 Kings 16:9). During that same period, Pekah was assassinated by Hoshea (732–722 B.C.), who succeeded him to the throne (15:30). According to Tiglath-Pileser's account, Hoshea was made king by the Assyrians and forced to pay a heavy tribute. Hoshea thus reigned over Israel as a vassal of Tiglath-Pileser and his successor, Shalmaneser V. In time, however, Hoshea stopped paying tribute to the Assyrian king and sought protection from Eygpt. That was a fateful decision, for Egypt proved ineffective against Assyria. The Assyrian army attacked Hoshea and placed him in prison (17:4). They besieged Samaria, his capital city, for three years, captured it in 722 B.C., and carried the inhabitants of the northern kingdom into captivity.

With the fateful reigns of Pekahiah, Pekah, and Hoshea, the northern kingdom of Israel came to a ruinous end. The Assyrian king who concluded the invasion may have been Sargon II, who replaced Shalmaneser V about this time.

The Successors to Rehoboam in the South

Abijah (1 Kings 15:1–8), the son of Rehoboam, succeeded his father to the throne. He reigned only three years (913–910 B.C.). Apart from the fact that he continued in the sins of his father and failed to trust in God wholeheartedly, little is known of his reign.

Asa, the son of Abijah (1 Kings 15:9–24), represented a turn for the better. He "did what was right in the eyes of the LORD, as his father David had done" (15:11). Consequently he gained the upper hand against the northern kingdom of Israel and enjoyed a good deal of peace with his neighbors. The only drawback to Asa's reign was his failure to remove the "high places" (15:14) from the northern kingdom, that is, he failed to remove the false worship centers at Bethel and Dan. The Bible mentions this not to find fault with Asa, but to reinforce the word of the man of God who had prophesied that Josiah would be the one to remove them (13:2).

Jehoshaphat (1 Kings 22:41–50), like his father Asa, was a good king. But also like his father, he did not remove "the high places" (22:43)—apparently the false worship centers at Bethel and Dan.

King Jehoram (Joram) (2 Kings 8:16–24), the son of Jehoshapat, married a daughter of the northern king Ahab. He thus followed the ways of the house of Ahab and proved to be a treacherous king. In his day the borders of the Davidic kingdom continued to give way to their surrounding enemies. The people of Edom, for example, rebelled against him and set up their own king (8:21).

Ahaziah (2 Kings 8:25–9:29), like his father Jehoram, was related to the house of Ahab. His mother was a granddaughter of King Omri (8:26; cf. 1 Kings 16:21–28). Ahaziah in fact, joined with Israel's king, Ahab's son Joram, in an unsuccessful attack on the Aramean king Hazael, who was threatening their northeastern borders. Because he was related to the house of Ahab, Ahaziah was killed by Jehu during his purge (2 Kings 9:27).

After Ahaziah's death, his mother, Athaliah, assumed the throne in Jerusalem and proceeded to destroy all possible rival heirs (2 Kings 11:1–3). But Joash (11:1–12:21), Ahaziah's son, was hidden away in the temple and remained there for a number of years (11:3, 21). When he was seven years old, Jehoiada, a priest at the temple, secretly executed a plan to make the young crown prince king and thus secure his rightful throne (11:4–21). The plan was successful and Athaliah was put to death (11:15–16).

King Joash to King Ahaz

Joash reigned for forty years. He was a good king. But he eventually fell prey to an assassination plot by two of his own officials (2 Kings 12:20). His son, Amaziah (2 Kings 14:1–22), succeeded him. Though Amaziah enjoyed considerable military success against the Edomites, he was defeated in battle by Jehoash, king of Israel (14:8–14), and, like his own father, fell prey to an internal conspiracy (14:19–20).

Amaziah's son Azariah (2 Kings 15:1–7), also called Uzziah, became king in his place. He was stricken with leprosy in the later part of his life (15:5). His son Jothan (742 B.C.) did what was right in the eyes of the Lord, that is, he obeyed the Torah and the word of the prophets (15:32–38). But like the kings of Judah before him, he did not remove the calf images and sanctuaries that Jeroboam had built in the northern kingdom. Jothan resisted an initial attack on his northern border from Israel's king Pekah and the Aramean king Rezin (2 Kings 15:37).

After Jotham's death (2 Kings 15:38), Ahaz (735–715 B.C.) became king of Judah (16:1–20). During his reign Pekah and Rezin attacked Jerusalem and besieged the city (16:5). Ahaz, a wicked king (16:2–4), appealed to the Assyrian king Tiglath-Pileser for help (16:7). The latter complied and, after being paid off with the silver and gold from the temple at Jerusalem (16:8), attacked and defeated Damascus (16:9; cf. Isa. 7:1–8:18).

While in Damascus with Tiglath-Pileser, Ahaz was impressed by a huge pagan altar he saw there. Sending a drawing of the altar back to Jerusalem, he commissioned the building of a similar altar and the reconstruction of the temple to accommodate it (2 Kings 16:10–18). This was a serious violation of the Mosaic commands that Solomon had so faithfully followed. On the eve of the fall of the northern kingdom, the kingdom of Judah was beginning to pick up where Jeroboam and the northern kingdom had left off—corrupting the true worship of God as prescribed in the Torah.

King Hezeiah

Hezekiah (2 Kings 18:1–20:21), the son of Ahaz, was king of Judah during the time the Assyrians attacked and deported the northern kingdom (18:9–12). Shortly after the fall of Samaria, Sargon II became the head of the growing Assyrian Empire (721 B.C.). Egypt too began to display increasing military might. Thinking Egypt might be strong enough to come to their aid, several of the western nations around Judah rebelled against the Assyrian rule. Hezekiah, however, did not join with them and thus escaped considerable ruin and destruction. Dependence on Egypt proved fatal for many of those nations.

During his reign, the Assyrians also invaded Judah and captured many of its cities (2 Kings 18:13), threatening even to lay siege to Jerusalem (18:14–19:34). But God intervened, and the Assyrians were severely and miraculously defeated (19:35–37).

Ancient historical sources have frequent references to events that transpired during the reign of Hezekiah. From the time of the fall of Samaria (722 B.C.) to the invasion of Judah by the Assyrian Sennacherib (701 B.C.), Judah's neighbors frequently rebelled against the Assyrians. At one point Hezekiah himself rebelled and cut off his payment of tribute to Assyria (18:7). Even though as a result Judah was invaded by the Assyrians and suffered much destruction, Hezekiah and Jerusalem remained unscathed.

Hezekiah is known for his extensive religious reforms. In the first year of his reign, he began to restore Judah's proper worship of the Lord (2 Chron. 29:3). He appointed the Levites to clean out the temple and offered many sacrifices at the altar to atone for Judah's many sins. He also sent agents throughout the land to tear down the high places and false worship centers that had been built by his predecessors (2 Kings 18:4).

During Hezekiah's reign, much work was carried out on the growing body of canonical Scripture. According to Proverbs 25:1, it was the "men of Hezekiah's" court who collected and edited the book of Proverbs. Early Jewish tradition also credits these scholars with the composition of the book of Isaiah.

The last years of Hezekiah's reign was a time of peace for the kingdom of Judah. It was, however, only the kind of peace that comes before a storm.

The Last Days of the Southern Kingdom

Manasseh (2 Kings 21:1–18), the son of Hezekiah, reigned from 687–642 B.C. He led the people in such apostasy that the Lord determined to bring destruction and exile on Judah and Jerusalem. The basis of God's complaint against Judah was their failure to keep the law of Moses (21:8–9). Even though Judah later repented and put away their idolatry (chs. 22–23), God did "not turn away from the heat of his fierce anger, which burned against Judah because of all that Manasseh had done to provoke him to anger" (23:26).

Manasseh's son Amon (2 Kings 21:19–26) was a carbon copy of his father. He fell victim to a conspiracy and assassination after only two years on the throne. His son Josiah (22:1–23:30) was a good king (22:1–2). He instigated the repair of the temple (22:3–7). In the process of cleaning the temple, the high priest, Hilkiah, found "the Book of the Law" (22:8), perhaps a copy of what we now have as the Pentateuch (cf. 23:25). When the book was brought before the king and read, it caused an instant revival (22:9–11). The king set out at once to obey what was written in the book and to avert the anger of the Lord so clearly spelled out (22:12–13). Josiah read the book before all the people (23:1–2), and they renewed their covenant with the Lord (23:3). All forms of pagan religion were removed from Jerusalem (23:5–7).

Josiah then sent word throughout his kingdom that all pagan worship was to be totally eradicated (2 Kings 23:8–20). As good as his reform was, it came too late. The coming exile foretold by Isaiah (20:16–18) could not be averted (23:26–27). Josiah himself was suddenly killed in a battle with the Egyptian Pharaoh Neco (23:29–30).

Josiah's son Jehoahaz (2 Kings 23:31–35) reigned only three months. He was imprisoned by Pharaoh Neco, who appointed Eliakim, another son of Josiah, as king, changing his name to Jehoiakim (23:36–24:7). During Jehoiakim's reign the Babylonian king Nebuchadnezzar first invaded Judah (24:1). Jehoiakim's son Jehoiachin reigned in Jerusalem only three months (24:8–25:30). He surrendered the city of Jerusalem to Nebuchadnezzar and his army (24:10–12a) and was taken prisoner to Babylon (24:12b, 15). He kept his title as "king of Judah" long after the Babylonian captivity (25:27–30). Nebuchadnezzar removed the royal treasures and temple artifacts to Babylon, along with all but the poorest inhabitants of the city. He made Mattaniah, Jehoiachin's uncle, king in Judah, changing his name to Zedekiah (24:17).

The Fall of Jerusalem

During the years of the decline of the southern kingdom of Judah, the political climate of the ancient Near East was considerably altered. The Assyrian empire, which had dominated world affairs in the ancient Near East since the days of Tiglath-pileser, began to fall apart. The newly emerging forces of the Neo-Babylonian empire broke free of Assyrian dominance under Nabopolasser in 626 B.C. In the following years, Babylon, with the help of the Medes, dealt a series of crushing blows to the Assyrian empire. In 612 B.C. Nineveh, the capital of Assyria, fell.

After the fall of Nineveh, the Assyrians, aided by the Egyptians, made one last, though unsuccessful, attempt to regain their glorious empire. They met the Babylonians in battle in Haran, a battle that lasted several months. En route to this battle Pharaoh Neco encountered the Judean king Josiah at Megiddo (2 Kings 23:29). He made quick work of Josiah when he refused to allow the Egyptian king to pass through Megiddo.

The Babylonians now controlled most of Mesopotamia, and they turned their attention westward to Syria and Canaan (Palestine)—the regions claimed by the Egyptians after the battle of Haran. The Egyptians met the Babylonians, led by a brilliant new commander, Nebuchadnezzar, in a fierce battle at Carchemish (605 B.C.), but they proved no match for the massive Babylonian forces. The control of Syria and Palestine passed to the Babylonians, and a number of Jewish people, including Daniel (Dan. 1:1–2), were carried into exile in Babylon. Nebuchadnezzar assumed the throne on September 7, 605 B.C.

In December 598 B.C. Nebuchadnezzar again moved his armies into Syria and Palestine, intent on punishing the rebellious King Jehoiakim at Jerusalem. He replaced him with his son Jehoiachin, who ruled only three months in Jerusalem (2 Kings 24:8). In March 597, Jehoiachin was taken captive to Babylon along with many others. Nebuchadnezzar placed Zedekiah on the throne. He was a son of King Josiah and a brother to both Jehoahaz and Jehoiakim. Nebuchadnezzar plundered the temple treasures at that time (24:13).

During Zedekiah's reign (2 Kings 24:18–25:7), Nebuchadnezzar again returned to plunder and destroy Jerusalem (25:1–10). The temple and the royal palace were burned, the walls were broken down, and most of the remaining people were taken into exile (25:11). The chief priests and the leading men of the city were executed (25:18–21). Nebuchadnezzar appointed Gedaliah over those who remained behind in Judah (25:22–25), but he was soon assassinated (25:25). Fearing Babylonian reprisals, the people fled to Egypt (25:26).

The Babylonian Exile

Life During the Babylonian Exile

Life in Palestine after the destruction of Jerusalem in 586 B.C. changed radically from what it had been. Archaeological evidence shows that every major city in Judah was destroyed at this time and was not rebuilt for many years. The entire population was killed in battle, died of starvation, or was deported to Babylon or Egypt. A few people remained settled in the northern parts of the land, for example, Samaria, Galilee, and to the east in the Transjordan. We read about those populations in the books that recount the events of the return from exile, but we know little about the lives of these people at this time.

Among those who fled to Egypt after the murder of Gedaliah was the prophet Jeremiah (cf. Jer. 42–44), taken to Egypt against his own will. He warned the people earnestly that they should stay in Judah and trust in the Lord to save them from Babylon. But the people did not heed his warning. There is considerable archaeological remains that relate to Jewish communities in Egypt. There was, for example, a thriving Jewish military colony in the fifth century B.C. at Elephantine, an island on the Nile that protected Egypt's southern borders.

The main center of Jewish life after the destruction of Jerusalem was, of course, Babylon itself. About 10,000 were taken into Babylon in 598 B.C. (2 Kings 24:14). Second Kings 25 does not give the number of Jews taken in the 586 B.C. exile; it states only that Nebuchadnezzar removed all those remaining in Jerusalem (25:11). Some were executed at Riblah, to the north of Jerusalem (25:18–21). According to Jeremiah 52:28–30, the number of male exiles for all of Nebuchadnezzar's campaigns was about 4,600. There was, then, a maximum of 20,000 exiles in Babylon (located in modern-day Iraq).

Once in Babylon, the Jewish exiles settled in their own territories, isolated from other populations. Ezekiel 3:15 tells of a settlement called Tel-Abib, which was beside the River Kebar, a tributary of the Euphrates River. (It was, in fact, in memory of that city that the modern city of Tel Aviv was built.) Ezra 2:59 and 8:17 also mention sites where the exiles settled in Babylon. The Jewish exiles were allowed to build houses and plant gardens (Jer. 29:5–6).

The Judean king Jehoiachin was treated with great respect, at least during the reign of the Babylonian king Evil-Merodoch. Jeremiah 29 and Ezekiel 8:1; 14:1; 33:30–32 give some information about the activities of the exiles. The only full account is the book of Daniel. (Esther is after the exile.)

The Last Days of the Babylonian Empire

After the destruction of Jerusalem in 586 B.C., Nebuchadnezzar continued to carry on military campaigns in Palestine. In 585 B.C. he besieged Tyre and blockaded the city for thirteen years (cf. Ezek. 26:7). Eventually, Nebuchadnezzar had to abandon his siege of the city because Tyre had moved to a more secure position on a nearby island fortress (cf. 29:17–20). In 582 B.C., Nebuchadnezzar again entered Palestine and carried off more exiles to Babylon (Jer. 52:30). In 568 B.C., he and his armies invaded Egypt.

After Nebuchadnezzar's death in 562 B.C., the massive power of the Babylonian empire began to break apart. Several weak kings ruled after him: Amel-Marduk (562–560 B.C.) or Evil-Merodach (2 Kings 25:27–30), Nergal-shar-usur (Neriglissar) (560–556 B.C.), and Labashi-Marduk (556/55 B.C.).

The last king of Babylon was Nabonidus (Nabu-na'id) (555–539 B.C.). He transferred his residence from Babylon to the Arabian desert oasis of Teima. He remained there ten years, leaving his son Belshazzar (Bal-shar-usur) in charge at Babylon. His own royal archives give an account of his entrusting the city "to his oldest son, the firstborn." For that reason Belshazzar is identified as the last king of Babylon in Daniel 5. In forsaking the city of Babylon and entrusting the kingship to Belshazzar, Nabonidus failed to appear during the annual New Year's Day rite in Babylon. Such an act of sacrilege within the religion of Babylon greatly angered the priestly leaders and ultimately led to their transfer of loyalty to the Persian king Cyrus.

The Medes and the Persians

The Medes and Persians are first mentioned in the historical records of the Assyrian king Shalmaneser III (836 B.C.). They were part of a large migration of Indo-Ayrian peoples from the northeast into the area that is now Iran. Shalmaneser III records that he received tribute from kings of "Parsua." These groups split into two larger groups, the Medes and the Persians. The Medes remained in the northern plateau area of Iran while the Persians moved south. These people became a unified group politically and militarily under the Median king Cyaxares (625–585 B.C.), who then formed a military alliance with the Babylonian king Nabopolasser. Together, the Medes and the Babylonians defeated the powerful Assyrian military by destroying their capital city, Nineveh, in 612 B.C. and the city of Haran in 610 B.C.

Following those successes, Cyaxares continued to extend his influence deep into Asia Minor. Astyages (585–550 B.C.) succeeded Cyaxares as king of Media. He gave his daughter, Mandane, to the Persian king Cambyses. From that marriage was born the Persian king Cyrus, later known as Cyrus the Great.

As one of his first acts, Cyrus (550–530 B.C.) gathered around himself the various independent Persian tribes and set out to conquer the Medes to the north, thereby laying the first stage of the Persian empire. He then turned his attention toward Asia Minor (547 B.C.); with the fall of the city of Sardis, Asia Minor fell into his hands. Cyrus's empire extended eastward as far as northwest India.

Cyrus then turned his armies against Babylon. He met with the Babylonian army at the central Mesopotamian city of Ophis, where one of his generals, Gobryas, defeated the Babylonians. In 539 B.C., the Persian army entered Babylon without resistance. Cyrus became emperor of the largest empire in history up to that time.

The Religious Policy
of the Persian Empire Under Cyrus

Cyrus promoted a kind of religious toleration within his empire. In one of his own inscriptions, for example, he says he daily worshiped the Babylonian god Marduk, even claiming that that god had appointed him to capture the city of Babylon and rescue it from the disastrous rule of the Babylonian king Nabonidus. In keeping with that policy, Cyrus issued an Edict of Restoration for the city of Jerusalem in the first year of his reign (Ezra 1:1), the purpose of which was to direct the rebuilding of the temple in Jerusalem: "The LORD, the God of heaven, has given me all the kingdoms of the earth and he has appointed me to build him a temple for him in Jerusalem" (1:2).

Such a statement prompts one to ask the extent to which Cyrus himself believed that Israel's God, the Lord, had given him all the kingdoms of the world. On the basis of the prophecies of Isaiah two hundred years earlier, we can say that, whether Cyrus knew it or not, the Lord, the Creator of heaven and earth, had given all the world into Cyrus's hand (Isa. 45:1–7). Moreover, the Lord appointed Cyrus to carry out his plan to rebuild his temple in Jerusalem (44:28). But 45:1–6 informs us that Cyrus himself did not acknowledge the Lord. The Lord, in other words, selected and used Cyrus, a pagan world leader, to carry out his specific plan for his chosen people Israel, just as he had done in selecting the Aramean king Hazael (1 Kings 19:15–16). When Cyrus spoke of being the Lord's "anointed one," carrying out the Lord's specific plans, he did not acknowledge the Lord as the true and only God.

Rather, Cyrus appears here to be merely claiming support for his political and religious policies from the God of those people for whom his policies applied. As just implied, Cyrus believed that Marduk had personally chose him to rule in Babylon after searching throughout all the countries for a righteous man willing to take the place of Nabonidus. In that inscription, Cyrus specifically claims that Marduk had given him rulership over all the world and told him to reestablish all the temples of the gods of Mesopotamia that Nabonidus had destroyed. Cyrus even concludes with a vow of worship and praise of this god of the Babylonians.

In sum, Cyrus' acknowledgment of Israel's God appears to have been part of a larger political strategy to mollify the nations whom the Babylonians had mistreated and deprived of a religious identity.

The Persian Empire After Cyrus

The Persian king who succeeded Cyrus was his son Cambyses (530–522 B.C.), who extended the Persian empire as far as Egypt. Returning from Egypt, Cambyses heard that rebellion had occurred in Persia and that someone calling himself Bordiya (Cambyses had killed his brother before the Egyptian campaign) had gained control. Cambyses died in Syria before he could return to suppress the rebellion. Darius (521–486 B.C.), one of Cambyses' bodyguards, returned to Persia and successfully put down the rebellion. He marched through Palestine in 519 B.C. and entered Egypt to assume full control there. Darius then completed an early version of a "Suez Canal," connecting the Mediterranean Sea with the Indian Ocean.

During the reign of Darius the Greeks first began to play a role in international affairs. Darius spent much effort establishing his borders on the eastern front of the Greek city-states. In 490 B.C. Darius fought the Greeks from Athens at Marathon and was defeated. Xerxes (cf. Est. 1:1), the son of Darius (486–465 B.C.), faced the major problem when he came to the throne of what to do with the rising power of the Greeks. In 480 B.C. he set out with a fleet of ships and successfully gained control of Athens and the Attican peninsula. In a foolish miscalculation, he reduced Athens to a fiery ruin. Such a provocative act united the Athenians and the other Greek city-states against the Persians. On September 22, 480 B.C., Xerxes' fleet was defeated by the Greeks in the narrow strait of Salamis, near the city of Corinth.

Xerxes spent his remaining years living in seclusion with his harem at Susa. During the last part of his reign, the events of the book of Esther occurred. His son Artaxerxes (465–424 B.C.) rose to the throne after Xerxes' murder. This was the Artaxerxes who allowed both Ezra to return to Jerusalem and his cupbearer, Nehemiah, to visit Jerusalem and repair its walls. Owing to increasing trouble on his western frontier, particularly in Egypt, Artaxerxes had a special interest in the political affairs of Palestine.

The Return From Babylonian Captivity

The Political Organization of Judah at the Time of the Return

At the time of the return of the exiles, Judah was a part of the Persian empire. This empire was divided into districts called *satrapies*. There were some twenty satrapies during the reign of Darius I, each of which was governed by an official called a satrap. Each satrapy was, in turn, divided into smaller provinces, each ruled by a governor. Palestine belonged to the satrapy called "Beyond the River." That satrapy included the regions of Syria, Phoenicia, and Palestine.

During the reign of Darius, Tattenai was satrap of "Beyond the River" (Ezra 5:3). The newly appointed governor of Judah was Sheshbazzar (5:14), known locally by the title "Prince of Judah" (1:8). Sheshbazzar was replaced by Zerubbabel as governor of Judah (cf. 3:2; Neh. 12:1; Hag. 1:1). Zerubbabel was the son of Shealtiel and thus was the grandson of King Jehoiachin (1 Chron. 3:17). In other words, Judah was granted the status of a province under the Persian empire and was governed by a descendant of the royal family of David.

One of the governors of Judah during the Persian period was a cupbearer named Nehemiah (Neh. 5:14, ca. 445–425 B.C.). The Elephantine papyri contain references to a Judean governor named Bagohi. The Bible also mentions several provinces bordering Judah at the time of the return from captivity (Neh. 2:19): the province of Samaria, governed by Sanballat during the time of Nehemiah; the province of Ammon, governed by Tobiah; the province of Arabia, governed by Geshem; and the province of Ashdod (governor unknown).

The First Stage of the Return

The first stage of the return from exile, recorded in Ezra 1:1–6:22, was the time of the building of the second temple. In 538 B.C. Cyrus, the emperor of Persia, issued his decree to rebuild the temple in Jerusalem (1:1–4; cf. 6:2–5). At that time the first group of Judeans left Babylon to return to Jerusalem. This group consisted of the "heads of the fathers of Judah and Benjamin," along with the priests and Levites who had been stirred up by God to go (1:5). The group was supported by a freewill offering from those Jews who remained behind. The group was accompanied by Sheshbazzar, appointed as the governor. Sheshbazzar had been entrusted with the articles of the temple that Cyrus was returning to Jerusalem (1:8).

At the same time, another group of 29,166 persons came from Babylon led by Zerubbabel (Ezra 2:2). There were also some from various places in Babylon who came but who were unable to give evidence of their family's genuine Israelite descent. They searched the ancestral records but could not verify their proper lineage (2:62). The priests among this group were prohibited from eating of the holy offerings until a decision could be reached regarding their lineage (2:63). According to 2:64, the total number of the whole assembly was 42,360.

In the seventh month of 538 B.C., all the returned exiles gathered in Jerusalem, and Jeshua the priest and Zerubbabel built an altar to offer burnt offerings (Ezra 3:1–3). They celebrated the Feast of Booths according to the Torah of Moses (3:4). In the second year of their return (536 B.C.), in the second month, Zerubbabel and Jeshua began the work of rebuilding the temple (3:8). Their first task was laying its foundation (3:11). When their enemies heard of the rebuilding of the temple, they wanted to help. Zerubbabel and Jeshua, however, refused the offer (4:3). Thereupon these enemies, the "people of the land," tried to discourage the building of the temple and were, in fact, successful until the time of the reign of Darius, sixteen years later (cf. 6:15; cf. 4:4–5). According to a parenthetical note inserted in 4:6–22, a similar effort on the part of Judah's enemies some seventy years later further hindered their rebuilding the city walls of Jerusalem.

The Restoration

Sixteen years after Zerubbabel and Jeshua had begun to lay the foundation of the temple, the prophets Haggai and Zechariah stirred up the people to continue that work (Ezra 5:1–2). Once again the satrap of "Beyond the River" tried to halt the building project by sending a letter to the Persian king, Darius. The letter requested confirmation of the permit given the Jews to rebuild the temple. This was, in effect, a request for a copy of the Edict of Restoration. Darius had the records searched in his capital city, Ecbatana, and a copy of the edict was recovered (6:1ff.). Darius thus commanded that the Jews be allowed to complete their work on the temple without interruption (6:7ff.). In the sixth year of Darius (516 B.C.), the temple was completed (6:15).

The events of the book of Esther fall between the building of the temple and the activities of Ezra—that is, between chapters 6 and 7 of the book of Ezra (a period of fifty-eight years). This was the time of the reign of the Persian king Xerxes (486–465 B.C.), a difficult time for the Persian empire. In 480 B.C., the Greeks had defeated the Persians at Salamis, and in 479 B.C. the Persians suffered further losses at Plateau. After that battle, Xerxes remained secluded in Susa, his capital, where we find him in the book of Esther.

Esther, also called Hadassah, and her cousin, Mordecai, were descendants of those Jews who had been taken into captivity in Babylon with Jehoiachin (597 B.C.). In the seventh year of Xerxes (479 B.C.), Esther entered his royal palace and was made queen of Persia (Est. 2:16–17)—the same year Xerxes returned from his devastating defeats by the Greeks.

The Second Stage of the Return

After the completion of the temple in the sixth year of Darius (516 B.C.), the Bible tells us nothing about what happened in Palestine for the next fifty-eight years. Some historians have suggested that the Jews who had earlier returned to Palestine with Sheshbazzar and Zerubbabel felt the impact of the decree of Xerxes ordering the death of all Jews and the seizing of their property (Est. 3:13). After this point, we no longer hear of Zerubbabel or any of the names of those who lived in Palestine. When Ezra returned to Judea from Babylon, he found a new generation of Jews in the land.

In the seventh year of his reign (458 B.C.), the Persian king Artaxerxes granted Ezra a special request to lead a group of Jews back to Jerusalem (Ezra 7:6–7). Ezra is described as a scribe, skilled in the law of Moses (7:6). He was a Levite and a descendant of Aaron (7:5), thereby qualified to function as a priest among the people. His mission in going to Jerusalem seems to have been to establish law and order in Judah as prescribed by the Torah (7:25–26). He was to appoint magistrates and judges to teach and enforce the Torah (7:25–26). Ezra was accompanied by 1,754 men (8:1–14).

Ezra's primary task in carrying out the demands of Torah was to deal with the problem of intermarriage by the Jews with foreign women (Ezra 9–10). According to Deuteronomy 7:3, the Israelites was forbidden to intermarry with the Canaanites. But those who returned to Judah had failed to keep that law and took foreign wives. Ezra recognized that intermarriage had been one of the leading factors that had led to Israel's and Judah's idolatry in the first place—for example, Solomon's wives and Ahab's wife Jezebel. Thus Ezra had to deal with this problem quickly and forthrightly (10:11). Those who had taken foreign wives were instructed to divorce them. When that injunction proved too complex to carry out, Ezra initiated a process of review whereby each case was dealt with individually.

The Third Stage of the Return

The events recorded in the book of Nehemiah occurred in the twentieth year of Artaxerxes I (445 B.C.)—that is, thirteen years after Ezra came to Jerusalem to set up the administration of God's law (Neh. 1:1). Nehemiah was a cupbearer to Artaxerxes at his palace in Susa (1:11). He heard a report that conditions were still grave for the returnees. The remnant was in great distress, the wall of Jerusalem had been "broken down," and the gates were burned (1:3; cf. 2 Kings 25). When Nehemiah heard that news, he lamented Jerusalem's trouble and prayed that God would remember his covenant and restore the city (Neh. 1:8ff.).

In that same year, Nehemiah received an appointment as governor of the province of Judah (Neh. 5:14) and was commissioned by Artaxerxes to repair the walls of Jerusalem (2:8). He traveled to Jerusalem with a written order from the king and accompanied by his army and cavalry (2:9). He met with immediate opposition from the other governors of "Beyond the River" (2:10, 19–20), such as Sanballat of Samaria and Tobiah of Ammon. Nehemiah and a small group of men secretly inspected the condition of the city walls at night. The following day, when he announced his plans to rebuild the wall, the Jews responded with great enthusiasm (2:12–18). The building plans, however, did not go unopposed. Sanballat, Tobiah, and other governors organized stiff resistance (4:7–8). Nehemiah armed his workers, and they completed the walls in fifty-two days without further incident (4:13–23; 6:1–15).

Following the completion of the city's walls, Ezra was asked to read the Torah before all the people (Neh. 8:1). Those who could not understand the reading had the passage explained to them by the priests who could understand (8:7). They thus heard the Torah "as it was made clear" to them (8:8). The people then celebrated the Feasts of Booths (8:13–18). As they gathered into a solemn assembly, they renewed their covenant with a vow to keep God's Torah (9:1–10:39). The walls were then dedicated (12:27) with singing and hymns of thanksgiving, accompanied by cymbals, harps, and lyres. Nehemiah had the leaders of Judah stand on top of the wall and arranged two large choirs, one to the right and one to the left, to march on top of the wall (12:3ff.). He also had two choirs in the temple area (12:40), where he himself stood with half of the officials (12:40). They sang and rejoiced and read the book of Moses aloud (13:1).

The Intertestamental Period

The Decline of Persia and the Rise of Macedon

Historians usually date the start of the decline of the Persian empire from the reign of Artaxerxes I (465–424 B.C.). This Persian king maintained power in the eastern half of his empire, but he gradually lost power in the western half (with the exception of keeping control over Egypt and Cyprus). During his reign and that of his successor, Darius II (424–404 B.C.), revolts continued at numerous places throughout the empire.

During the time of Artaxerxes II (404–358 B.C.), conflicts continued with the Greek city-states. These were finally resolved in a treaty known as "the King's peace" (386 B.C.), in which Artaxerxes maintained power over the Greek city-states of Asia Minor but ceded all the rest either to Athens or to independent status. Persia was given the responsibility for enforcing this decision, which allowed it to interfere in Greek politics. Egypt also fought for and achieved independence during Artaxerxes' reign.

Artaxerxes II was succeeded by his son, Artaxerxes III (358–338 B.C.). He was determined to reassert Persian power and managed to put Egypt once again under Persian control. He concluded an alliance with Athens to keep influence on the Greek peninsula, but this alliance was nullified when Philip of Macedon defeated the Athenians. The growing power of Macedonia coincided with the continuing decline of Persia after the death of Artaxerxes III.

The same year that Darius III (336–330 B.C.) ascended the throne in Persia, Alexander the Great came to power in Macedonia, with a commission from his father, Philip, to make war on the Persians. After securing his power on the Greek mainland, Alexander crossed over into Asia Minor. Darius, thinking he would have an easy victory, sent an army against Alexander, but it was soundly defeated at Granicus River. This opened the door to the East for Alexander.

Alexander the Great

Alexander's first task was to bring Asia Minor under his control, which he accomplished in short order. His major battle was at Issus (333 B.C.), the city to which Darius III had advanced with his Persian army, hoping to stop the Macedonian general. Instead, Alexander won a decisive victory, even capturing the family of Darius.

Rather than continuing to advance eastward against the Persian king, Alexander turned south to Phoenicia, Palestine, and Egypt. Except for the cities of Tyre and Gaza, he won easy victories, especially since he was seen as a liberator from the power of Persia. After firmly establishing his power in these areas, Alexander then headed east toward Persia. He resisted the efforts of Darius to negotiate a treaty of land and money for peace and the return of his family. In 331 B.C., at Gaugamela in the Mesopotamian plain, Alexander and Darius met again in a fierce battle. The Persian army was soundly defeated, and there was nothing left to stop Alexander from taking the capital cities of the Persian empire—Babylon, Susa, Persepolis, and Ecbatana. By 330 B.C., Darius III was dead and Alexander was king of the world.

Alexander continued to push east, going to the borders of India. But resentment toward his rule was building in areas already conquered, and he had to turn more and more attention to consolidate his rule and put out fires of rebellion. In 323 B.C., at age thirty-three, Alexander died from a fever. His only heir was a son born after his death.

In all of his conquests, Alexander the Great was determined to spread the glories of Greek culture, in which he himself had been trained. He encouraged his army officers to mingle with the conquered nations and marry local women. This spread of the Greek way of life and thinking is probably his greatest legacy, since within a couple centuries of his death, the cultural language spoken throughout the territory he conquered was Greek. This age is known by historians as the Hellenistic Age (*Hellenas* is the Greek word for "Greece").

Seleucids, Ptolemies, and Antigonids

Since Alexander the Great left no heir who could take charge of his empire, several of his capable generals vied to be his successor. By the time the dust settled on all the alliances, counter-alliances, and battles, Antigonus and his successors controlled Macedonia, Seleucus and his successors controlled Syria and Asia Minor, and Ptolemy and his successors controlled Egypt and Palestine. Things did not remain static, however, as the Ptolemies and Seleucids continued to battle each other for more power and control in the border areas (especially Palestine).

In 223 B.C., Antiochus III (the Great) came to the throne of Syria. He was determined to take Palestine from the Ptolemies and annex it to his kingdom. During most of his reign (223–187 B.C.), he fought numerous battles, and Palestine changed hands several times (the history of the conflict between these two dynasties and kingdoms is foretold, in an apocalyptic manner, in Daniel 11). In 198, at a crucial battle at Panias (Caesarea Philippi in the New Testament), Antiochus III defeated Ptolemy IV and his general Scopas. This battle marked a turning point for the Jews, for from this point on until Roman control began in 63 B.C., the Jews in Palestine remained under Seleucid rule.

Antiochus then decided to expand his kingdom into Greece, where he was met by the powerful Roman armies. After his defeat and retreat, he had to pay an enormous indemnity and give up part of Asia Minor to the Romans. In order to enforce the payment of the indemnity, the Seleucid king had to supply his victors with twenty hostages, one of which was his own son, Antiochus Epiphanes (who eventually became Antiochus IV). In Rome, this young man learned respect for Roman power and the Roman way of doing things.

The Ptolemies had been tolerant of the Jewish religion, but the Seleucids were determined to require the Jews to accept Hellenism. This process reached its apex during the reign of Antiochus Epiphanes.

Antiochus IV Epiphanes

Soon after Antiochus IV came to the throne (175 B.C.), he was called upon to settle a dispute between two Jewish brothers (Onias and Jason), both of whom wanted to be high priest in Jerusalem. Onias was a strict orthodox Jew and favored the Ptolemies, whereas Jason was sympathetic to the Seleucid program of Hellenization. Furthermore, Jason promised to pay a higher tribute to Antiochus than Onias. Consequently, Antiochus appointed him as high priest, and Jason instituted several steps to introduce Hellenism to the Jews (such as building a gymnasium in Jerusalem in order to train Jewish youth for Greek games) and to "modernize" Judaism. Antiochus looked on Hellenization as a way of integrating the Jews into his empire socially and therefore unifying the empire.

Three years later, however, a certain Menelaus (not at all from the priestly line) offered Antiochus an even higher tribute than Jason and a more vigorous Hellenization program, and Antiochus appointed him high priest. In order to meet his financial commitments, he had to plunder the temple of some of its treasures, which led to fierce resistance and even riots on the part of the Jewish masses. Jason gathered together an army from Transjordan, where he had fled, and attacked Jerusalem. After limited success, he was defeated and fled again across the Jordan.

Rome now had conquered Macedonia and Egypt, and Antiochus was desperate for Palestine to be a buffer zone between the growing power of Rome and his own capital. He thus organized an attack on Jerusalem on the Sabbath (168 B.C.), knowing that the Jews would not fight. He killed many men, women, and children and set out, in a cruel manner, to exterminate the Jewish religion by outlawing its unique practices (such as circumcision, sacrifices, and festivals). In its place, everyone in his empire was required to worship the Greek gods. He had a bearded image of Jupiter placed in the temple in Jerusalem, and pigs were sacrificed on the altar of burnt offering. All copies of the Torah were ordered destroyed (see Dan. 11:29–31).

But Antiochus, with this consistent program of Hellenization, underestimated the power of the Jews and the Jewish religion. His actions sparked a fierce rebellion, begun in the town of Modein (seventeen miles northwest of Jerusalem) by a certain Matthaias and his sons, who eventually became known as the Maccabees.

The Maccabees

Antiochus IV required every town in Palestine to set up an altar to Zeus and to offer unclean sacrifices. In Modein, Matthaias (a priest and leader of the village) was ordered to set an example by offering the first sacrifice, but he refused (168 B.C.). When another Jew offered to be the first, Matthaias killed him and the legate of Antiochus and tore town the altar. He then fled into the mountains with his five sons and many other followers. There they organized themselves into an army and began a campaign of guerrilla warfare. Their first ventures were in Jewish towns that had followed Antiochus's program of Hellenization, where they tore down altars, circumcised children, and encouraged Jews to join their cause.

In 166 B.C., the aged Matthaias died, but his five sons continued the struggle, led by the middle son, Judas (Maccabaeus). Their forces grew to the point where they were able to engage the Syrian armies of Antiochus in open battle, and they were victorious. In 165 B.C., Judas and his men liberated the city of Jerusalem, selected priests loyal to Israel's God, destroyed the altar of Zeus in the temple, and rebuilt the altar of the Lord. This marvelous event is still celebrated by the Jews in the Festival of Hanukkah.

Religious freedom was not sufficient for the Maccabees, however. They wanted political freedom and continued the struggle, especially after the Syrians managed to get Alcimus, a Hellenizing priest, installed as high priest. In the ensuing battle, Judas was killed, and it was left to his youngest brother, Jonathan, to take up the torch of freedom.

By this time, Antiochus IV was dead, and a power struggle developed between Demetrius II (his rightful heir) and Alexander Balas. Jonathan and his troops sided with Alexander, who won the struggle. Jonathan was then installed as high priest (c. 150 B.C.), and he also sought political aid from Rome to keep Syria at bay from any further interference. When Jonathan was assassinated in an act of political treachery, his brother Simon (second oldest in the family and now an old man) took over as priest and leader of the people (143 B.C.). During his tenure, the legitimacy of his priesthood was accepted by all Jews (including the Hasidim ["the pious ones"], who had been strong supporters of the Maccabees but who until then recognized the family of Onias as the rightful heirs to the high priesthood). That dynasty was known as the Hasmoneans.

The Hasmoneans

The first of the Hasmoneans, John Hyrcanus (ruled 135–104 B.C.), entered into a political agreement with the reigning Syrians. He ceded to Syria control over certain coastal cities that the Maccabees had won and promised political allegiance to Syria; in exchange, the Syrians agreed not to interfere in the internal affairs of the Jews. As a result, the Hellenizing party disappeared from influence in the Jewish political scene.

The Hasmonean rulers, even though they were high priests, concentrated their efforts in politics and military affairs rather than in religious issues. Hyrcanus himself attempted to regain control over the coastal cities he had given up. He also annexed Idumea, where the descendants of the Edomites were living. Hyrcanus's successor, his son Aristobulus, took for himself the title "king"; he reigned for only one year. He was followed by his brother, Alexander Jannaeus (103–76 B.C.), who expanded his territory to include almost the entire area ruled by David and Solomon. Internally, however, he had severe conflicts with the Pharisees, which eventually erupted into a six-year civil war. Alexander came out the winner and instigated cruel vengeance on the Pharisees.

Alexander was succeeded by his widow, Salome Alexandra (also widow of Aristobulus). During her seven years in power there was relative peace. She appointed her son Hyrcanus as high priest and another son Aristobulus as military commander. During this time, the Pharisees were able to exert considerable influence and decreed that every Jewish boy should be educated in the Hebrew Scriptures. But the Sadducees were not pleased with their decreasing power, and they rallied around Aristobulus. After Alexandra died, the conflict between the two brothers, Hyrcanus and Aristobulus, broke out into the open in a civil conflict that involved the Idumeans and Nabatean Arabs; it was not resolved until the Romans, led by Pompey, intervened.

The Jews Under Roman Rule

The Roman general Pompey decided to throw his weight behind Hyrcanus. After a three-month siege of Jerusalem, Aristobulus capitulated and Pompey entered the Holy City and the temple (including the Most Holy Place). In contrast to many other rulers, however, Pompey did not plunder the temple but allowed Jewish worship to continue. Judea now became a part of the Roman province of Syria. Pompey installed Hyrcanus as ethnarch of Judea and high priest of the Jews (63–40 B.C.)

During Hyrcanus's tenure, the Idumeans gained a great deal of power in Jewish politics—much to the displeasure of conservative Jews, who viewed these descendants of the Edomites as godless rivals. Antipater, governor of the Idumeans, had rallied to support Hyrcanus against Aristobulus, and as a reward he received an increasing influence in Jewish affairs. Since he had risked his life for Caesar in Egypt, the Romans named Antipater "Procurator of Judea." Ultimately, he was the power behind Hyrcanus.

After Antipater died (43 B.C.), his son Herod grew in power and influence. He was engaged to a granddaughter of Hyrcanus, Mariamne, which strengthened his claim to the Hasmonean throne. After numerous political intrigues and visits to Rome, Herod received wholehearted support for his political ambitions and was named "King of the Jews." In 37 B.C. he managed, with the help of Roman troops, to drive the last of the Hasmoneans from Jerusalem. He endeared himself, at least partially, to the Jews by personally paying off the Roman soldiers so that they did not plunder the temple.

This Herod, known as Herod the Great, was ruler of the Jews at the time Christ as born. He engaged in numerous lavish building projects, including the temple in Jerusalem (see John 2:20). He also gained favor with the Jews by twice lowering their taxes. But he was also known, especially toward the end of his life, for extreme cruelty, including the murders of several of his sons, who were beginning to vie for power in the event of his death; he also had Miriamne killed. His cruelty is memorialized in Scripture in the deaths of the infants in Bethlehem at the birth of Jesus (Matt. 2:16–18). Herod died in 4 B.C., and his kingdom was divided up among three of his sons—Philip, Archelaus, and Antipas.

Judaism in the Intertestamental Period I

Several significant developments took place in Judaism during the intertestamental period. The first was the establishment of the synagogue. Tradition places the origin of the synagogue during the Babylonian exile, when the Jews, now without a temple, turned to a study of their Scriptures and prayer as the focal point of their relationship with God. Even after the Return and the rebuilding of the temple, many Jews remained dispersed throughout the world, and regular meetings around the Scriptures fulfilled their spiritual needs. Even in Palestine, the temple became the place of sacrifices and festival celebrations, but the synagogue remained the place of prayer and the study of Torah.

The leadership of the Jews fell not only to the high priest but also to local bodies of elders. In larger towns, a body of elders (from seven to twenty-three men) formed the Sanhedrin or the governing body of the synagogue. This body served as a court, which adjudicated religious and even sometimes civil affairs. It could sentence flogging, though its highest form of punishment was excommunication from the Jewish community (*herem*). The body of elders in Jerusalem was known as the Great Sanhedrin, which had seventy members and was presided over by the high priest.

In general, synagogues were constructed so that their entrance faced Jerusalem. The focal point of the sanctuary was the "ark," which contained the Torah and other sacred writings. In the center was the raised platform (the *bema*), which contained a lectern for the public reading of the Scriptures.

In most services, the Scriptures were read in Hebrew and then translated into the language of the common people, Aramaic. But as a result of the Hellenization of Judaism, the Scriptures were also translated in Greek (a translation called the Septuagint, done in Alexandria, Egypt). Also in Egypt, biblical interpreters used Greek methods of interpreting sacred texts, called allegory. The most famous of these was Philo of Alexandria, who lived in the first century A.D.

Judaism in the Intertestamental Period II

During the intertestamental period, various sects arose within Judaism, mostly as a result of the impact of Hellenization. Many Jews were willing to tolerate a synthesis of Greek civilization with their religion, but (as noted above) some reacted violently against Hellenizers. These latter were known as the Hasidim (meaning "the pious ones"). Their cause was eventually championed by the Pharisees (meaning "separated ones").

The Pharisees stood against political leaders such as John Hyrcanus, who had combined the role of high priest and civil leader; they also resisted the mixture of Greek and Jewish ways of life. Religiously, the Pharisees concentrated on interpretating the Torah, trying to help the people understand God's will for their lives in a changing society. Two schools of legal thought developed: the school of Hillel, which was more moderate in legal interpretations of the Old Testament, and the school of Shammai, which was more strict.

Like the Pharisees, the Essenes continued the tradition of Hasidim. But they withdrew from involvement in regular Jewish life to form separate monastic-like communities. Many think that the community of Qumran, from whom we have received the Dead Sea Scrolls, was an Essene community. The Essenes were ascetic in lifestyle, insisted on strict discipline in their communities, and enforced a literal interpretation of God's law.

The Sadducees formed the wealthy Jewish aristocracy and by and large favored Hellenization. They controlled the high priesthood and administered the temple. They owed their power to the Romans. Politically and religiously, therefore, they were at odds with the Pharisees. When Jerusalem was destroyed in A.D. 70, their party ceased.

Jewish hatred for Roman rule of Palestine led to the formation of the party of the Zealots. These political and religious extremists refused to pay taxes to Rome and to acknowledge loyalty to any ruler over Israel except the Lord God. They did not hesitate to use violence to achieve their objectives and played a significant role in the defense of Jerusalem in the Jewish-Roman war of A.D. 66–70. After Jerusalem fell, most of the Zealots were killed and the movement eventually died out. One of Jesus' disciples, Simon, is called a "Zealot" (Mark 3:18).